HALO

ESCALATION

Illustration by Daniel Chavez

ESCALATION

VOLUME 3

SCRIPTS
DUFFY BOUDREAU

PENCILS
SERGIO ARIÑO
DOUGLAS FRANCHIN

INKS
JUAN CASTRO
ROB LEAN
DENIS FREITAS
DOUGLAS FRANCHIN

COLORS
MICHAEL ATIYEH

LETTERING
MICHAEL HEISLER

COVER ART
JEAN-SÉBASTIEN ROSSBACH

DARK HORSE BOOKS

PUBLISHER
MIKE RICHARDSON

COLLECTION DESIGNER
SANDY TANAKA

DIGITAL PRODUCTION
RYAN JORGENSEN

ASSISTANT EDITORS
EVERETT PATTERSON
ROXY POLK

EDITOR
AARON WALKER

HALO: ESCALATION Volume 3

This volume collects issues #13–#18 of the Dark Horse comic book series *Halo: Escalation*.

Special thanks to Christine Finch, Nicholas Gallagher, Kevin Grace, Tyler Jeffers, Scott Jobe, Carlos Naranjo, Tiffany O'Brien, Frank O'Connor, Jeremy Patenaude, Kenneth Peters, Brian Reed, Corrinne Robinson, Sparth, and Kiki Wolfkill at Microsoft.

Published by
Dark Horse Books
A division of Dark Horse Comics, Inc.
10956 SE Main Street
Milwaukie, OR 97222

DarkHorse.com
HaloWaypoint.com

First edition: September 2015
ISBN 978-1-61655-759-1

1 3 5 7 9 10 8 6 4 2
Printed in China

Illustration by Jean-Sébastien Rossbach

THE UNITED NATIONS SPACE COMMAND (UNSC) is a surviving military offshoot of the United Nations, now utilized by the Unified Earth Government (UEG) for the deployment of military and exploratory assets.

THE FORERUNNERS were an ancient race of advanced beings. Long extinct, the Forerunners have left hidden treasures of technology scattered throughout the galaxy.

THE COVENANT is an alliance of alien species who worship the Forerunners as gods and are hell bent on the destruction of humanity. Shattered by civil war, the Covenant rises again under the leadership of Commander Jul 'Mdama.

THE YEAR 2258: The Forerunner shield world of Requiem is gone, but the secrets it contained continue to live on. Shortly before the planet's destruction, the brilliant Dr. Catherine Halsey—creator of the Spartan supersoldiers and Cortana—recovered an artifact from its depths known as the Janus Key, a piece of Forerunner technology of unprecedented power . . .

FROM THE PERSONAL RECORDINGS OF
DR. CATHERINE HALSEY
2558-07-15
THE KEY TO OUR FUTURE LIES IN OUR PAST.
LUCKILY, THOSE WHO CAME BEFORE US -- THE ONES WE CALL FORERUNNERS -- HAVE PROVIDED US A PASSPORT INTO THIS PREVIOUSLY IMPENETRABLE WORLD.

THE REMNANTS OF THEIR CIVILIZATION ARE NOT MERE MONUMENTS TO THE GREATEST INTELLIGENCE TO EVER INHABIT OUR UNIVERSE.
THEY ARE GIFTS.

OBJECTS OF ASTOUNDING COMPLEXITY AND ELEGANT SIMPLICITY.
UNLOCKING THE POTENTIAL OF THESE ARTIFACTS COULD VERY WELL CHANGE OUR CONCEPTION OF LIFE ITSELF.

AND THOUGH I MAY INDULGE IN A CERTAIN *AWE* WHEN CONSIDERING THE LIMITLESS POSSIBILITIES OF *TOMORROW'S* WORLD, I HARBOR NO ILLUSIONS AS TO OUR *CURRENT* REALITY.
I'VE SEEN FAR TOO MUCH OF WHAT *IT* HAS TO OFFER...
THE AGGREGATION OF POWER FOR ITS OWN SAKE.
INANE SUPERSTITION COUPLED WITH A SELF-FULFILLING PROPHECY OF ANNIHILATION.
OUR CONFRONTATION WITH THIS ANIMAL BRUTALITY LEFT US WITH VERY FEW OPTIONS...
IT'S BECOME QUITE... FASHIONABLE... TO CONDEMN THE UNSAVORY ORIGINS OF MY NOW-NOTORIOUS *SPARTAN-II* PROJECT.
BUT WITHOUT THAT PROGRAM -- AND THE CONTRIBUTION OF *ONE* SPARTAN IN PARTICULAR -- HUMANITY WOULD HAVE BEEN COMPLETELY WIPED FROM EXISTENCE.
THE HYPOCRITES WHO RUN THE UNSC *KNOW* THIS.
THEIR RELIANCE ON POOR COPIES OF MY WORK IS *PROOF* OF ITS VALUE.

AS PROUD AS I AM OF THAT CONTRIBUTION, I NOW KNOW IT WAS ONLY A STEP TOWARD SOMETHING MUCH LARGER.
AN OPPORTUNITY I'D NEVER EVEN IMAGINED...
UNTIL I CAME FACE TO FACE WITH ONE OF THE ANCIENTS. A FORERUNNER KNOWN AS LIBRARIAN.
SHE KNEW MY NAME AND SPOKE OF MY DESTINY... AN IMPENDING JOURNEY TO A PLACE CALLED THE ABSOLUTE RECORD.
WAITING FOR ME THERE -- A MAP, UNLIKE ANY OTHER, PROVIDING THE REAL-TIME LOCATION OF EVERY PIECE OF FORERUNNER TECHNOLOGY HIDDEN THROUGHOUT THE UNIVERSE.
THEN SHE ENTRUSTED ME WITH THE JANUS KEY -- THE ARTIFACT THAT UNLOCKS THE RECORD.
THE ARTIFACT THAT GRANTS ACCESS TO ALL OTHERS.

I'M EXPERIENCING A SLIGHT DELAY IN MY JOURNEY TO THE RECORD. FOR THAT, I HAVE ONLY MYSELF TO BLAME.
YES, THE CIRCUMSTANCES WERE EXTREME, BUT MY ACTIONS WERE RASH.
I MADE THE ERROR OF MISTAKING AN ENEMY FOR AN ALLY.
THORNE! TAKE THE KEY!
I NO LONGER THINK IN SUCH SIMPLISTIC TERMS.
NOW, THERE IS ONLY THE OBJECTIVE.
REUNITING THE KEY. FULFILLING LIBRARIAN'S INSTRUCTION.
I WAS ONCE ASKED WHAT I WANTED OUT OF LIFE, AND I REPLIED -- "TO KNOW EVERYTHING."
LOOKING BACK, IT'S ALWAYS SEEMED A RATHER DRAMATIC, EMOTIONAL RESPONSE.
BUT AS I STAND HERE NOW, AFTER EVERYTHING I'VE SUFFERED...
I THINK IT'S A PERFECT ANSWER.

JOINT SPARTAN-UNSC MARINE OPERATION
NORTHEASTERN SAVIRON, OBAN
2558-07-16

THORNE!

THANKS, COMMANDER.
PROMETHEAN KNIGHTS?
I KNEW IT. I KNEW HE WAS HERE...

LISTEN UP! THIS IS COMMANDER PALMER.
I WANT ALL TEAMS ON THE LOOKOUT FOR JUL 'MDAMA...

YOU SHOULD ALL ALREADY KNOW HOW TO I.D. HIM, BUT I'M SENDING HIS IMAGE AGAIN.
I REPEAT, COVENANT LEADER AND HIGH-VALUE TARGET 'MDAMA IS LIKELY SOMEWHERE IN THE VICINITY.

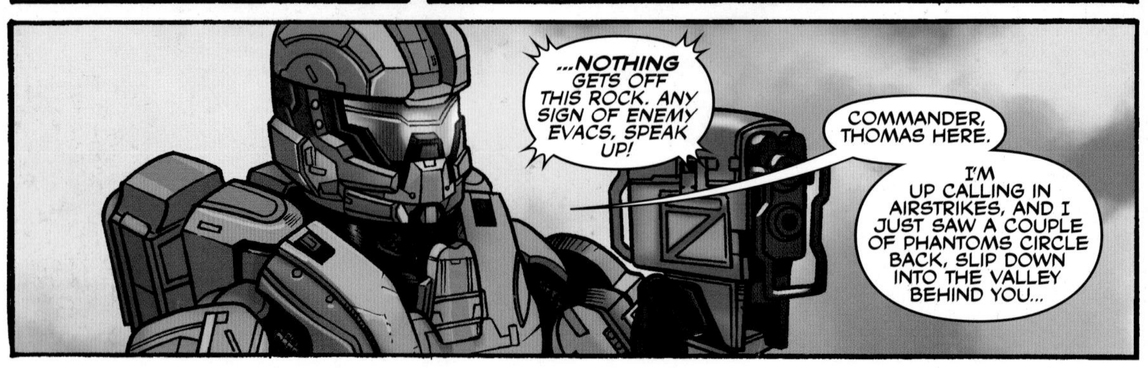

...NOTHING GETS OFF THIS ROCK. ANY SIGN OF ENEMY EVACS, SPEAK UP!
COMMANDER, THOMAS HERE.
I'M UP CALLING IN AIRSTRIKES, AND I JUST SAW A COUPLE OF PHANTOMS CIRCLE BACK, SLIP DOWN INTO THE VALLEY BEHIND YOU...

...BUT WE SHOULD HAVE IT COVERED. I JUST SCRAMBLED A LONGSWORD...
YOU HEAR THAT, THORNE? LET'S GET TO THE TRUCK!
HE JUST SAID AIR SUPPORT'S --
TO THE *TRUCK,* THORNE!
CRAWLERS!
SKREEEE
BRAKKA BRAKKA BRAKKA
THOOM-THOOM
THOOM THOOM THOOM
BRAKKA
I'LL DRIVE! YOU HOP UP ON THAT GUN!

ALL DUE RESPECT, COMMANDER, I'M NOT SURE WHAT WE'RE RUSHING OFF TO ACCOMPLISH.
I'M NOT TAKING ANY CHANCES.
IF JUL'S HERE, HE'S NOT GETTING AWAY.

WHOA-WHOA-WHOA!

HEY! DON'T SPEED UP! THE HELL ARE YOU DOING?!

THUNK

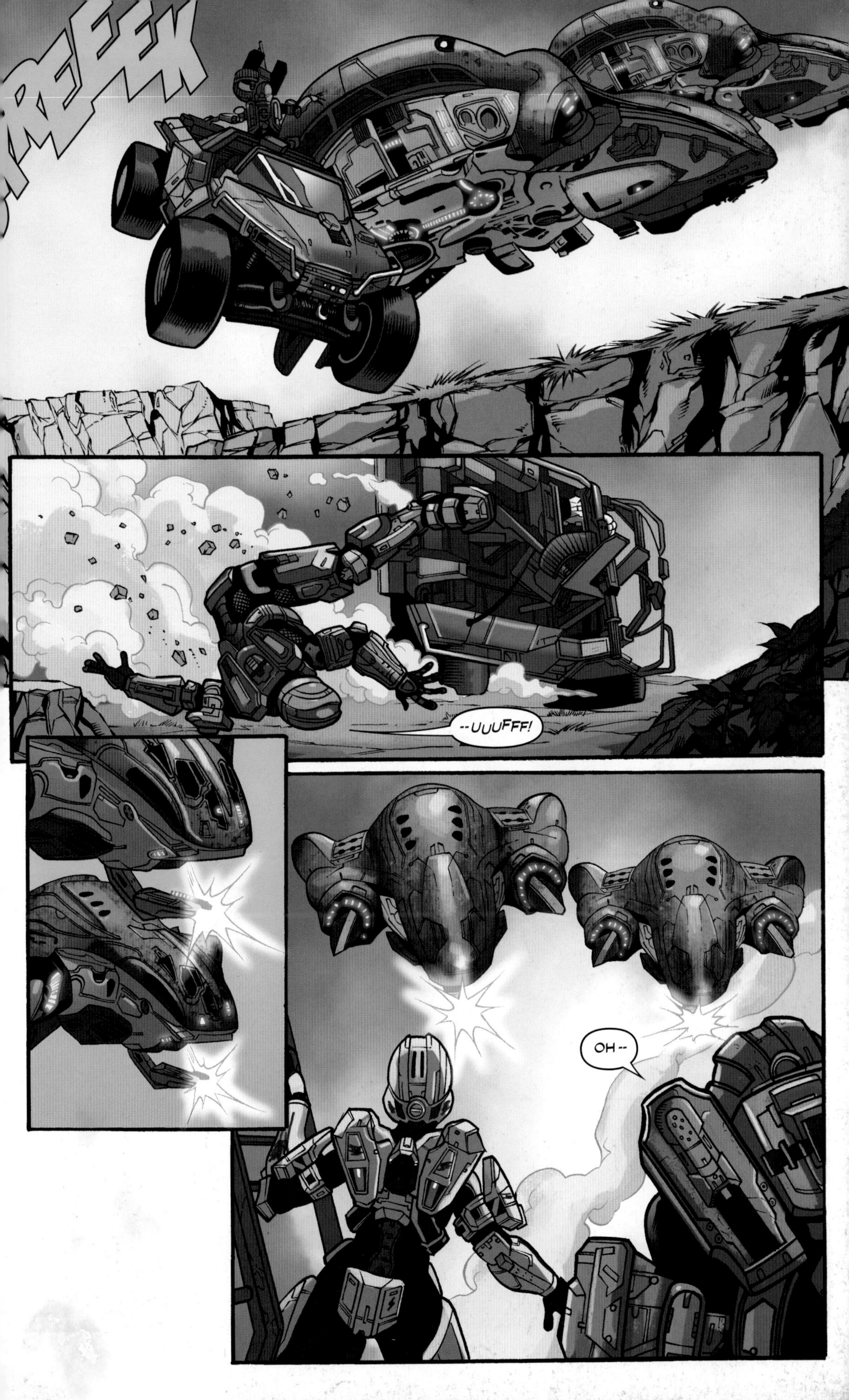
REEEK
--UUUFFF!
OH --

KA-THOOM
KA-THOOM

THOMAS! THIS IS PALMER!
MAKE SURE YOUR BIRD KNOWS HE HAS FRIENDLIES ON THE GROUND DOWN HERE!
HE KNOWS, COMMANDER. WE ALL SAW YOU CHARGING IN.

DAMN. I REALLY WISH YOU *HADN'T.*
YOU OKAY, THORNE?
YEAH...I... *THINK* I...FEEL EVERYTHING...

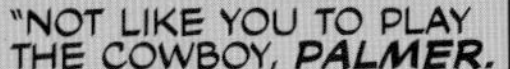
"NOT LIKE YOU TO PLAY THE COWBOY, PALMER.

UNSC INFINITY
"SPARTAN LIFE TOO BORING FOR YOU THESE DAYS, OR YOU GOING THROUGH SOME MIDLIFE CRISIS WE NEED TO TALK ABOUT?"

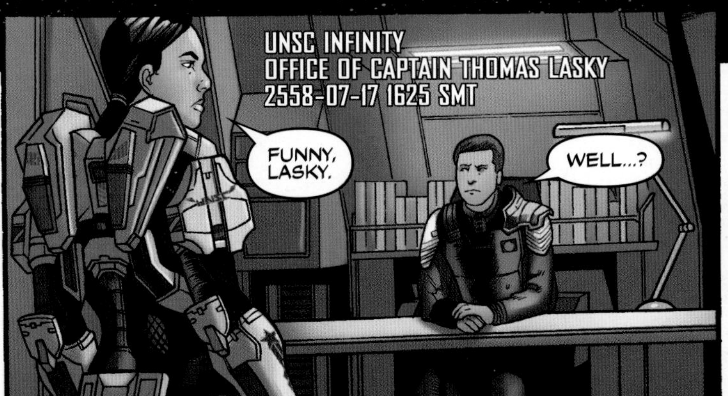
UNSC INFINITY
OFFICE OF CAPTAIN THOMAS LASKY
2558-07-17 1625 SMT
FUNNY, LASKY.
WELL...?

WHAT DO WE KNOW ABOUT THE ATTACK ON OBAN?
WHY WOULD THE COVIES TARGET SOME FRONTIER TOWN FULL OF ENGINEERS AND CONSTRUCTION WORKERS?

TO DESTROY THE NEW POWER STATION, DISRUPT OUR COLONIZATION EFFORTS THERE...
BUT I SEE WHAT YOU'RE SAYING.
HARD TO UNDERSTAND WHAT JUL GETS OUT OF THIS IN THE LONG RUN. PAID AN AWFULLY HEAVY PRICE TO DO JUST A BIT OF DAMAGE.

AND NO SIGN OF HIM AMONG THE WRECKAGE?
NO, BUT WE NEVER HAD ANY PROOF HE WAS ON THE GROUND IN THE FIRST PLACE.
AS MUCH AS CERTAIN PEOPLE CONVINCED THEMSELVES OTHERWISE...

BUT ALL THIS FRUSTRATION'S NOT REALLY ABOUT JUL, IS IT?
IT'S ABOUT CATHERINE HALSEY.

THAT'S WHY YOU WANT HIM SO BAD. BECAUSE ONE LEADS TO THE OTHER.

IT STILL BURNS, TOM.
THIS WOMAN, SUPPOSEDLY THE GREATEST SCIENTIFIC MIND OF HER GENERATION, IS OUT THERE COLLAB-ORATING WITH THE ENEMY.
ALL BECAUSE WE FAILED TO DO OUR JOB.

I'M THE ONE WHO PULLED HER OUT OF CONFINEMENT. AND ALL THE... *COMPLICATIONS*...THAT FOLLOWED...THOSE WERE COMPLETELY ON ME.
I'M DESPERATE TO GET HER BACK IN CUSTODY, TOO.
BACK IN *CUSTODY?*

OBVIOUSLY WE'VE GOT RADICALLY DIFFERENT IDEAS OF THE *OBJECTIVE* HERE, CAPTAIN.
I ALREADY SAID I MISSED MY SHOT *ONCE.* THAT'S NOT A VIABLE EXCUSE ANYMORE.

PALMER--
HALSEY WAS A WAR CRIMINAL. NOW SHE'S A TRAITOR AND A TERRORIST.
I GET HER IN MY SIGHTS, SHE'S GOING DOWN.

UNSC INFINITY
RESEARCH LABORATORY 3C
2558-07-18 1840 SMT

WHAT *ARE* YOU?
WHAT *IS IT* YOU WERE DESIGNED TO *DO?*

THOUGHT IT WAS TO KILL COVIES, BUT APPARENTLY I NOW ALSO DOUBLE AS THE WORLD'S MOST EXPENSIVE MESSENGING SERVICE.

OH. PALMER.
WE CALLED DOWN HERE TWICE ALREADY, DR. GLASSMAN.
I SHUT OFF MY COMMS. DIDN'T WANT TO BE DISTURBED.

I NEED THAT FINAL HEAD COUNT FOR THE *GALILEO II* SURVEY TEAM.
I'M PUTTING YOUR SECURITY ESCORT TOGETHER NOW AND DON'T HAVE MUCH TIME. WE'RE ABOUT TO ENTER SLIPSPACE. HEAD TO A POTENTIAL BASE SITE.

READY
CONSIDERING THE FATE OF THE FIRST LAB, IT'S FUNNY HIGH COMMAND SETTLED ON *GALILEO II* AS THE NAME OF THEIR NEW PREMIER RESEARCH BASE.
PERSONALLY, I DON'T NEED A DAILY REMINDER OF THE DISASTER OF REQUIEM.
ACTIVA

WE SHOULDN'T JUDGE THE REQUIEM CAMPAIGN UNTIL WE GET A MORE COMPLETE UNDERSTANDING OF THE ***ARTIFACTS*** WE DISCOVERED THERE.
WELL, THE PRIMARY ARTIFACT WE DISCOVERED THERE TETHERED US TO THE PLANET AND ALMOST GOT US INCINERATED BY ITS SUN. WHAT'S THIS ONE DO?

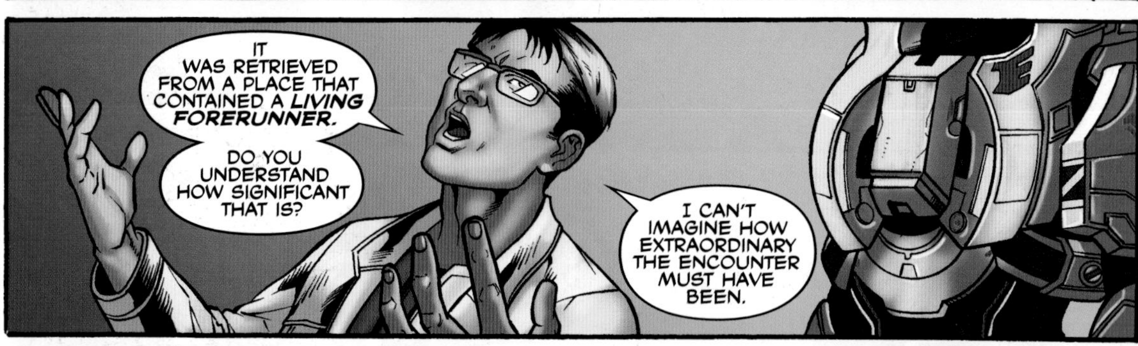
IT WAS RETRIEVED FROM A PLACE THAT CONTAINED A ***LIVING FORERUNNER.***
DO YOU UNDERSTAND HOW SIGNIFICANT THAT IS?
I CAN'T IMAGINE HOW EXTRAORDINARY THE ENCOUNTER MUST HAVE BEEN.

OF COURSE, I SHOULDN'T HAVE TO. DR. HALSEY ***COULD*** HAVE TOLD US ALL ABOUT IT.
THAT IS, BEFORE JUL KIDNAPPED HER. OR SHE DEFECTED. OR WHATEVER THE LATEST OFFICIAL VERSION OF THE STORY IS.

TRULY UNCANNY, YOUR ABILITY TO LOCK SO PRECISELY ONTO THE ***ONE*** SUBJECT GUARANTEED TO PISS ME OFF TODAY.

JUST SAYING. I DON'T WANT TO MAKE ANY MISTAKES MYSELF.
END UP ON YOUR HIT LIST.

"NOT TO WORRY, GLASSMAN. YOU'LL NEVER BE ON THAT LIST.
"YOU'RE NOWHERE ***NEAR*** IMPORTANT ENOUGH."

I WONDER...
ALL RIGHT, LET'S CUT THE CRAP.
JUST GIVE ME FINAL NUMBERS FOR YOUR TEAM AND I'LL GET OUT OF --
AAAAAAAH!
READY

UNSC INFINITY

SHE'S LOOSE!

SKREEEEEEEEE

TONNGGGG

KRUNCH

"THE HELL'S GOING ON, ROLAND?!
"DID WE JUST EXIT SLIPSPACE?"
WHEE-OOOP WHEE-OOOP WHEE-OOOP WHEE-OOOP WHEE-OOOP WHEE-OOO
We did, Captain. Right into an asteroid field.
I'm running a damage assessment...
WHILE YOU'RE AT IT, KILL THE ALARM. I'M PRETTY SURE EVERYONE'S AWAKE NOW.
A couple of wrecked Pelicans and a fire in one of the deployment bays...
Multiple injuries reported, but no major damage.
WE'RE DAMN LUCKY.
THAT COULD HAVE BEEN CATASTROPHIC.
It must have been an engine malfunction...
...But everything seems to be in order and back online. We should be good to proceed.
PUT ME THROUGH TO THE SHIP'S MAIN COMMS.
LISTEN UP, PEOPLE. THIS IS CAPTAIN LASKY.
UNBELIEVABLE AS IT MAY SOUND, INFINITY IS INTACT AND WE ARE PREPARED TO PROCEED. WE'LL BE RE-ENTERING SLIPSPACE SHORTLY.
IN THE MEANTIME, I'LL HAVE MED CREWS AVAILABLE TO DEAL WITH ANY CASUALTIES.

"I've reconfirmed the coordinates, Captain. We're good to go."
"OKAY, ROLAND. LET'S DO IT..."
"What the...?"
"DID WE JUST FALL OUT OF SLIPSPACE AGAIN?
"HOW FAR DID WE GET THIS TIME?"
A quarter of a kilometer, Captain.
I'm not sure what's going on...
WELL, GIVE ME SOMETHING, ROLAND.
"I wouldn't advise initiating another jump, sir. Who knows how far we'll get? And if we end up back in the rocks, we probably won't be as fortunate as last time."
"ROLAND, TELL COMMANDER PALMER TO GRAB DR. GLASSMAN...

"...I NEED THEM BOTH IN THE *ENGINE ROOM* NOW."
THIS DOESN'T MAKE ANY SENSE...
WHAT DO WE PAY YOU FOR AGAIN, GLASSMAN?
DIDN'T YOU HELP INSTALL THESE ENGINES?
YES, BUT LIKE I'VE SAID BEFORE, THIS IS AN ALIEN TECHNOLOGY...
...ENGINEERED ONE HUNDRED THOUSAND YEARS AGO AND GRAFTED ONTO THE SHIP BY A MAD SCIENTIST. WE GET THAT, DOCTOR.
BUT SINCE OUR MAD SCIENTIST IS MISSING, WE'RE RELYING ON *YOU* TO FIX THIS.
ANYTIME I ENTER FRESH COORDINATES, THE ENGINES OVERRIDE THEM. AUTOMATICALLY DEFAULT BACK TO RANDOM LOCAL ADDRESSES.
BASICALLY, WE'RE STUCK IN A SLIPSPACE CUL-DE-SAC.
Not sure if it's relevant, Captain, but I've detected an unusually strong energy reading nearby...

We're in an uncharted system, but here's what I've pieced together from preliminary scans.
The increased energy levels look to be emanating from a spot along this planet's equator.

COULD THAT BE THE SOURCE OF OUR PROBLEM?
HARD TO SAY...IT'S POSSIBLE.

WE'RE SURE AS HELL NOT MAKING ANY PROGRESS HERE.
I'LL GET A TEAM TOGETHER, HEAD DOWN THERE, AND CHECK IT OUT.

YOU THINK IT'S SMART TO RUN A RECON MISSION WITH INFINITY HOBBLED?
I DON'T SEE A PROBLEM WITH IT. THE SHIP'S STILL FULLY STAFFED AND ARMED.
SO LONG AS GLASSMAN'S STUMPED, I THINK IT'S OUR BEST OPTION...

"LASKY'S HEADING TOWARD THE *SIGNAL.*"
"IT *WORKED?*"
HOW?
THIS ARTIFACT YOU EXTRACTED FROM REQUIEM HAS PROVEN ITSELF OF GREAT VALUE, *JUL.*
IT'S ENABLED ME TO COMMUNICATE DIRECTLY WITH *INFINITY'S* FORERUNNER COMPONENTS AND SCRAMBLE THE SHIP'S SLIPSPACE COORDINATES.
LUCKY FOR YOU, *HALSEY...* AFTER THE DEFEAT AT OBAN, MY LIEUTENANTS WERE CALLING FOR YOUR HEAD.
WE HAD TO MAKE A BOLD MOVE AGAINST THE *UNSC.* IT WAS THE ONLY WAY TO DRAW *INFINITY* CLOSE ENOUGH FOR ME TO ESTABLISH THE INITIAL LINK BETWEEN THE ARTIFACT AND THOSE ENGINES.
A SACRIFICE MORE THAN JUSTIFIED BY OUR CURRENT POSITION.
NOW WE DON'T EVEN HAVE TO CHANCE A DIRECT ATTACK ON *INFINITY.*
WE'LL SIMPLY WAIT FOR THEM TO TAKE THEIR HALF OF THE KEY *OFF* THE SHIP...
AND DELIVER IT DIRECTLY TO *US.*

INCIDENT REPORT: 2558-07-18/19
1840 SMT: During the course of a survey mission, the UNSC *Infinity* abruptly fell out of slipspace, landing in an uncharted area beyond the Outer Colonies.
1845: Subsequent attempt to initiate slipspace jump failed. Engine malfunction became apparent, though its origin remained unidentified.
2030: Captain Thomas Lasky deployed a recon team to investigate a potential source of interference emanating from a nearby planet -- provisionally designated Aktis IV.
2345: Aktis IV exhibited habitable conditions upon initial atmospheric assessment.
Surface imagery revealed a vast ocean of an opaque, foamy substance. It is of unknown composition and largely impenetrable to radar analysis.
0130: The energy emissions in question led to an equatorial archipelago, the exact source pinpointed on the chain's northern end.

0245: Covenant forces identified at point of interest. Spartan Commander Sarah Palmer requested permission to engage.
HOPE SOMEBODY'S COVERING MY LEFT FLANK...
"...'CAUSE WE'VE GOT A RUNNER HEADED STRAIGHT FOR THAT PLASMA CANNON."
I'M ON IT, COMMANDER.
PTHEW
THWOP
AK!
NO! NO! NO!

GOOD WORK, RAY.
I THINK THAT'S ALL OF 'EM.
THOOOOM!
CAPTAIN LASKY, YOU COPY?
WE DID...
FIND ANYTHING INTERESTING DOWN THERE, COMMANDER?
A COUPLE OF RECENTLY UNEARTHED FORERUNNER STRUCTURES.
COVIES LEFT A REAL SKELETON FORCE DOWN HERE TO GUARD THIS DIG.
PROBABLY THOUGHT THE SITE WAS FAR ENOUGH OFF THE MAP WE'D NEVER FIND IT.
WE CAUGHT THEM OFF GUARD, BUT AN ALARM MAY HAVE BEEN TRIPPED.
KEEP AN EYE OUT. CAVALRY MIGHT BE ROLLING IN ANY SECOND.
ALREADY ON IT.
GOOD. I'LL PULL GLASSMAN OFF THE PELICAN, HEAD DOWN FOR A LOOK...

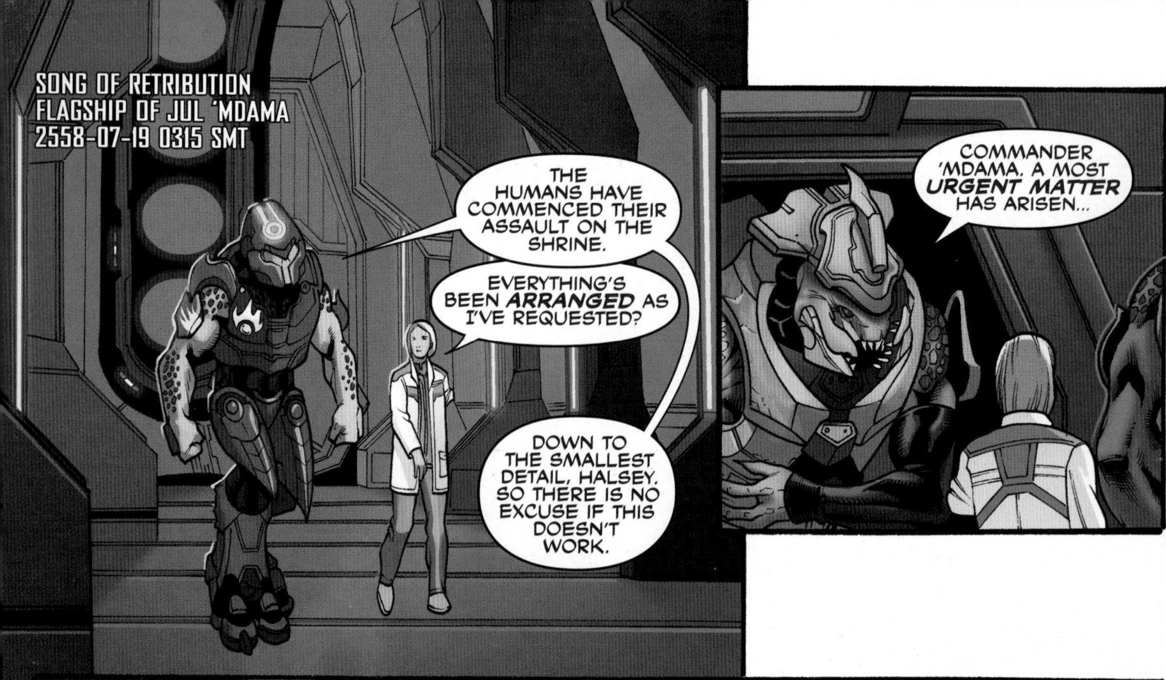
SONG OF RETRIBUTION
FLAGSHIP OF JUL 'MDAMA
2558-07-19 0315 SMT
THE HUMANS HAVE COMMENCED THEIR ASSAULT ON THE SHRINE.
EVERYTHING'S BEEN ARRANGED AS I'VE REQUESTED?
DOWN TO THE SMALLEST DETAIL, HALSEY. SO THERE IS NO EXCUSE IF THIS DOESN'T WORK.
COMMANDER 'MDAMA, A MOST URGENT MATTER HAS ARISEN...

IT PAINS ME TO SPEAK OF IT, BUT WE HAVE IDENTIFIED A CIRCLE OF TRAITORS WITHIN OUR RANKS.
WHEN WE MOVED AGAINST THEM, SOME ESCAPED, OTHERS WERE KILLED.
WE CAPTURED THIS ONE, WHO HAS BEEN BUSY FOR SOME TIME NOW TRYING TO RECRUIT OUR BROTHERS INTO HIS BLASPHEMOUS CAUSE.

HE CLAIMS THE HAND OF THE DIDACT IS A FALSE PROPHET.

REMOVE HIS MUZZLE.

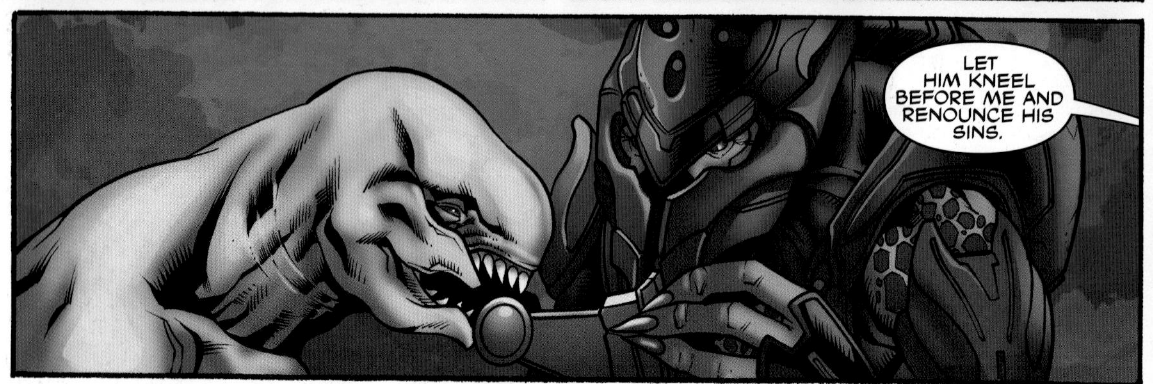
LET HIM KNEEL BEFORE ME AND RENOUNCE HIS SINS.

I RENOUNCE NOTHING.
IT IS YOU WHO SHOULD RENOUNCE.
YOU ALLOWED REQUIEM, THE HOLIEST OF SITES, TO BE ANNIHILATED.

AND NOW YOU RECEIVE COUNSEL FROM A FILTHY HUMAN.
SHE IS POISON, SENT TO DESTROY US FROM WITHIN.

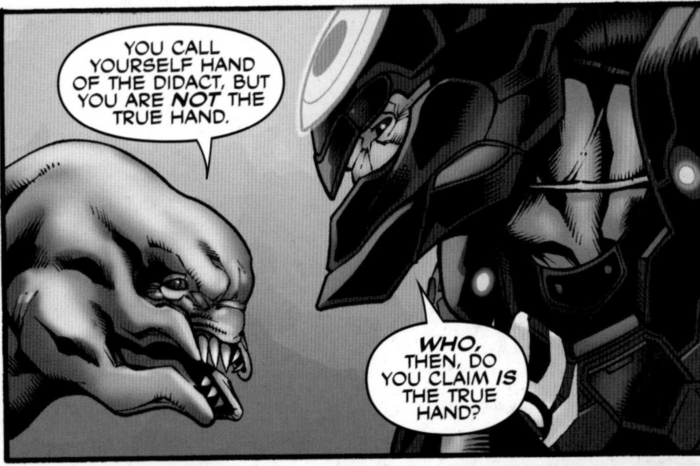
YOU CALL YOURSELF HAND OF THE DIDACT, BUT YOU ARE NOT THE TRUE HAND.
WHO, THEN, DO YOU CLAIM IS THE TRUE HAND?

HIS HOLINESS, SALI 'NYON.

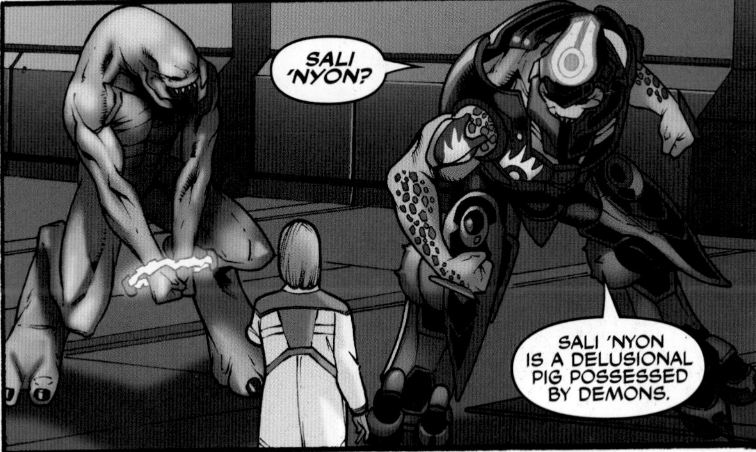
SALI 'NYON?
SALI 'NYON IS A DELUSIONAL PIG POSSESSED BY DEMONS.

NO! HE IS BLESSED AND HAS BEEN BROUGHT TO THIS UNIVERSE TO DEPOSE ALL USURPERS --

HRUPF--
BROTHERS, IF YOU HEAR EVEN THE *SLIGHTEST* RUMOR OF BLASPHEMY, I ORDER YOU TO UNDERTAKE THE NECESSARY ACTIONS YOURSELVES.
ALL HERETICS ARE TO BE ELIMINATED IMMEDIATELY. THEY SHALL RECEIVE NO FURTHER AUDIENCE WITH ME.
I'M GLAD TO SEE YOU APPRECIATE THE NATURE OF OUR SITUATION, JUL...
THAT THERE ARE MORE PRESSING MATTERS THAN THESE LITTLE *POLITICAL* DISTRACTIONS.

HOYA, YOU STAY ON THE ENTRANCE. I WANT THORNE AND RAY ON THE NORTH AND EAST WALLS.
I'LL SHADOW GLASSMAN.
INITIAL THOUGHTS, DOCTOR?
THE SITE'S PROBABLY PART OF A TRANS-LOCATION GRID. ONCE I ACCESS THE TERMINAL I SHOULD KNOW MORE.
THE GRID ITSELF SHOULDN'T BE THE SOURCE OF OUR PROBLEM.
BUT THAT DOESN'T MEAN THAT SOMETHING ELSE DOWN HERE ISN'T PRODUCING THE INTER-FERENCE...
IF WE GET STUCK, WE CAN ALWAYS JUST SHUT IT ALL DOWN. HOW LONG YOU THINK IT'LL TAKE TO KILL THE POWER?
GLASSMAN?

DAMMIT, GLASSMAN.
DON'T DISAPPEAR ON ME LIKE THAT.

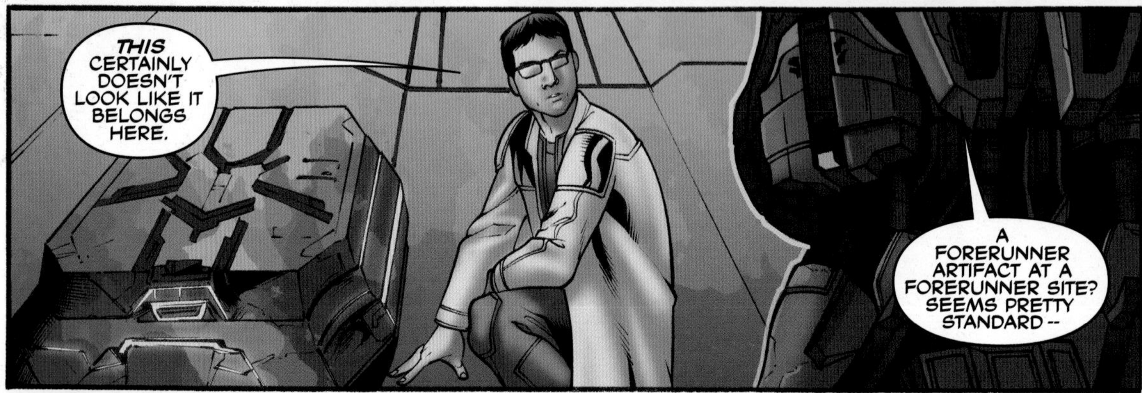
THIS CERTAINLY DOESN'T LOOK LIKE IT BELONGS HERE.
A FORERUNNER ARTIFACT AT A FORERUNNER SITE? SEEMS PRETTY STANDARD --

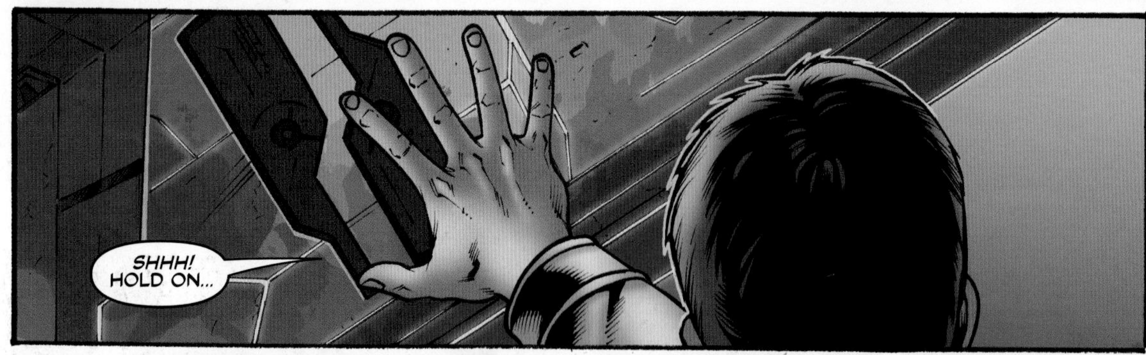
SHHH! HOLD ON...

THE SHAPE OF THESE INDENTATIONS IS FAMILIAR, ALMOST EXACTLY LIKE...

"...THAT ARTIFACT WE RECOVERED FROM REQUIEM. THE KEY."

GLASSMAN'S TAKING THE BAIT.
THE DECOY ARTIFACT WE COBBLED TOGETHER CERTAINLY SERVED ITS PURPOSE.
SO IT DID. BUT LET THIS BE THE LAST TIME WE SPEAK OF THE EXTREME METHODS EMPLOYED IN THIS MOST DIRE MATTER...
THE FABRICATION OF FALSE ARTIFACTS IS SACRILEGE.
ONE DOES NOT MAKE IMPERFECT COPIES OF PERFECT OBJECTS.
REALLY, JUL. IT'S JUST THE TWO OF US IN HERE.
YOU CAN EASE UP ON THE CLOYING DISPLAYS OF PIETY.
WHA--?
I KNEW THEY'D NEVER SUSPECT A TRAP. IT'S BEEN OVER FIVE MONTHS SINCE REQUIEM.
WITH EVERYTHING THE UNSC'S DEALT WITH SINCE THEN, THE KEY IS THE LAST THING ON THEIR MINDS...
NOT ONE OF THEM HAS AN INKLING OF HOW IMPORTANT IT REALLY IS.
EXCEPT FOR HENRY GLASSMAN.

I SEE WHAT YOU'RE THINKING AND THE ANSWER IS *HELL NO.*
NO WAY WE'RE HAULING THIS THING ABOARD *INFINITY.*

IT DIDN'T EVEN CROSS MY MIND, PALMER.
THE LAST THING I NEED IS ANOTHER MYSTERY ARTIFACT WREAKING HAVOC UP THERE.

BUT I DO HAVE TO EXAMINE IT, SEE HOW IT INTERACTS WITH THE KEY.
I CAN RUN ALL THE NECESSARY TESTS ONSITE, WHILE I'M TROUBLE-SHOOTING.

HMM. YOUR PLATE'S LOOKING FULL ENOUGH AS IT IS, DOCTOR.

HAVE LASKY SHUTTLE THE KEY AND A FEW SMALL PIECES OF MOBILE LAB EQUIPMENT DOWN HERE. THAT'S ALL I'M ASKING.
I PROMISE IT WON'T CAUSE ANY SIGNIFICANT DELAY.

PLEASE...

CAPTAIN, PALMER HERE. GOT KIND OF A STRANGE REQUEST FOR YOU...
THIS IS IT.
I'LL SEND OUT THE SIGNAL, PUT ALL TEAMS ON HIGH ALERT.
A WORD OF *CAUTION,* JUL...

"YOUR FORCES MUSTN'T MOVE UNTIL THE KEY'S LANDED SAFELY. UNDER NO CIRCUMSTANCES CAN IT BE ***DAMAGED.***
UNSC

"THE FIRST STAGE OF THIS OPERATION WILL REQUIRE EXTREME ***PRECISION.***

"***AFTER*** WE'VE TAKEN POSSESSION, HOWEVER, RESTRAINT WILL NO LONGER BE REQUIRED."

UNSC INFINITY
2558-07-19 0817 SMT
PACKAGE IS WRAPPED UP NICE AND SNUG, CAPTAIN.
GOOD. LOAD IT.
ANY LUCK WITH THE ENGINES, ROLAND?
I'm running a maintenance program to recalibrate the system. If that doesn't work, I'm not sure what's next.
WELL, LET'S HOPE GLASSMAN COMES UP WITH *SOMETHING.*
All due respect, Captain -- shouldn't Glassman's sole focus right now be to identify potential sources of interference? Sending the artifact down there could be a distraction.
PALMER PROMISED ME SHE'D KEEP HIM ON TASK.
WHO KNOWS, THE TWO THINGS MAY EVEN BE RELATED.
IT WON'T COST US ANYTHING TO LET HIM TINKER WITH THE KEY.
NOT LIKE WE'RE ON A SCHEDULE HERE. WE HAVE ALL THE *TIME* IN THE WORLD...
"ONLY THING WE'RE SHORT OF RIGHT NOW IS *SOLUTIONS.*"

AKTIS IV
2558-07-19 1145 SMT
WANTED TO SEE ME, COMMANDER?
THORNE, THE PELICAN CARRYING GLASSMAN'S TOYS LEFT INFINITY ABOUT THREE HOURS AGO. IT'LL BE CRUISING IN ANY MINUTE.
WHEN THE MATERIALS ARRIVE, YOU'RE IN CHARGE OF GETTING THEM DOWN TO SITE.
PALMER. LASKY HERE. YOUR PELICAN'S INBOUND NOW...
UNSC
YOU SHOULD BE ABLE TO SPOT HER. APPROACHING FROM THE SOUTH, COMING IN LOW WITH A BROADSWORD ESCORT...
YEP. HERE THEY ARE.
WHILE WE'RE WAITING, TELL ME SOMETHING GOOD, PALMER -- LIKE THIS DETOUR ISN'T GONNA BE A TOTAL BUST.
LOOK AT IT THIS WAY, CAPTAIN: EVEN IF GLASSMAN DOESN'T PULL ANYTHING VALUABLE FROM THE SITE, AT LEAST WE'LL HAVE THE SATISFACTION OF LEVELING THE PLACE. THAT SHOULD PUT A SMILE ON YOUR --

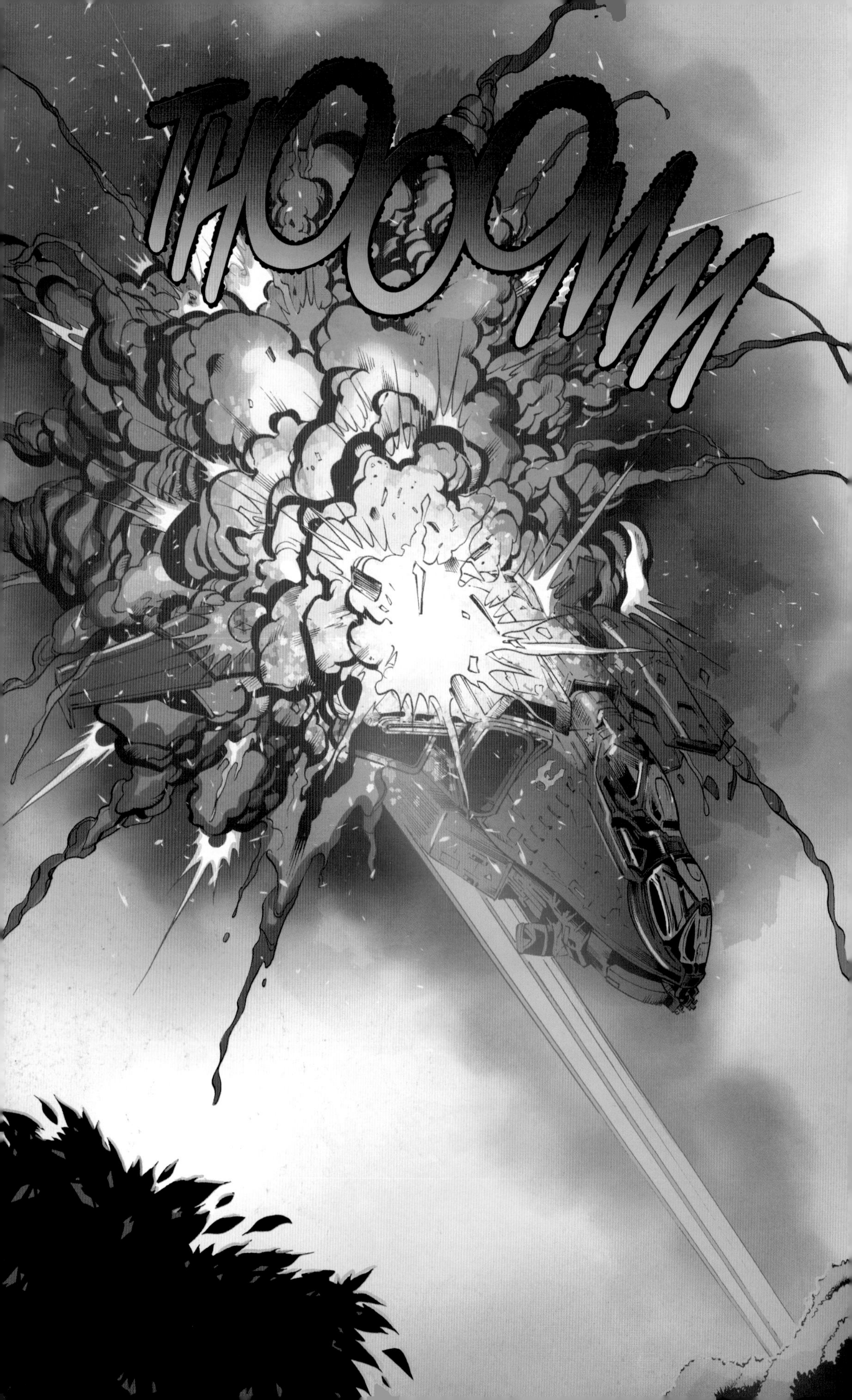
THOOOMM

THE HELL WAS THAT?!
THE PELICAN'S BEEN HIT! THERE'S --
BROADSWORD'S HIT TOO!
THOOOM
WHAT'S GOING ON DOWN THERE, PALMER?!
AA FIRE, BUT I CAN'T TELL WHERE IT'S COMING FROM!
PELICAN'S MAKING A CRASH LANDING...
I JUST LOST IT IN THE TREES!

SONG OF RETRIBUTION
2558-07-19 1147 SMT
WHAT HAVE YOU DONE!
I TOLD YOU TO WAIT UNTIL THE ARTIFACT WAS OFF THE SHIP!
I...I DID NOT...
I GAVE NO ORDER TO ATTACK!
WHO FIRED THOSE SHOTS?!
IT COULD NOT HAVE BEEN OUR FORCES. WE HAVE NO UNITS IN THAT POSITION.
BUT IN LIGHT OF THIS UNFORTUNATE INCIDENT, COMMANDER, SHALL WE STILL PROCEED WITH THE OPERATION?
YOU'LL DO NOTHING OF THE SORT! YOU MUST REPOSITION THE FLEET FIRST, DRAW THE UNSC'S FOCUS AWAY FROM THE CRASH SITE!
QUIET!
I AM THE COMMANDER OF THIS SHIP! IT IS MY DECISION, NOT YOURS!
THE ORIGINAL PLAN IS A BUST, JUL! SURELY EVEN YOU CAN SEE THAT!

BREATH OF ANNIHILATION
COVENANT ASSAULT CARRIER
2558-07-19 1149 SMT
COMMANDER...
UNITS ON THE GROUND ARE REPORTING SHOTS FIRED. IS THIS TRUE?
TWO UNSC SHIPS WERE JUST ATTACKED.
YET COMMANDER 'MDAMA'S SIGNAL HAS NOT YET ARRIVED.
IT WAS MOST LIKELY THE RESULT OF AN IMPULSIVE ACTION, FROM A UNIT UNDER OUR DIRECT COMMAND.
BUT THAT HAS YET TO BE CONFIRMED.
CONFIRMED OR NOT, THE BLAME WILL FALL ON US.
WE'LL BE THRASHED WHEN THE COMMANDER LEARNS OF THIS. IF HE HASN'T ALREADY...
NOTHING SHORT OF TOTAL VICTORY CAN SAVE US NOW, BROTHER.
LET US HOPE THAT WE ARE BLESSED.
RELAY THE ATTACK SIGNAL!
MOVE THE FLEET TO SURFACE POSITIONS!

CAPTAIN, THIS IS GROUP ONE LEADER.

SOUND THE ALARM AND SADDLE UP...

THERE'S ABOUT TO BE A HELLUVA LOT **MORE** TROUBLE DOWN HERE.

PALMER, YOU HEAR THAT?
IT'S ALREADY ARRIVED ON MY END, CAPTAIN.
WE'RE TAKING HEAVY FIRE FROM POSITIONS IN THE HILLS.
COVIES MUST HAVE BEEN WATCHING US THE WHOLE DAMN TIME.
CAN YOU GET TO GLASSMAN?
YEAH, BUT WHAT ABOUT OUR WOUNDED BIRD?
YOU'RE SPREAD TOO THIN FOR A SEARCH AND RESCUE. PULL BACK INTO THAT FORERUNNER SITE AND DEFEND.
"HOLD THEM OFF AS LONG AS YOU CAN, PALMER.
"WE'RE INBOUND NOW. I'LL HAVE A FULL FORCE ON THE GROUND IN NO TIME."

WE'RE *MOVING?* PLEASE TELL ME YOU'VE DECIDED TO REPOSITION THE FLEET.

IT IS TOO LATE FOR THAT. THE HUMANS HAVE DISCOVERED OUR PRESENCE.

HOW? HOW DID THIS HAPPEN?

WHAT *HAS* HAPPENED IS NOT MY PRIMARY CONCERN...

WE STILL HAVE A MASSIVE ADVANTAGE. IF WE MOVE QUICKLY, WE WILL HAVE THE AREA COMPLETELY SURROUNDED BY THE TIME THE REST OF THE HUMAN FORCES ARRIVE.

IF FULL-SCALE WAR BREAKS OUT WE'LL NEVER RECOVER THE KEY!

GIVE ME A TEAM AND I'LL SCOUR THE CRASH SITE MYSELF.
PLEASE...

YOU WILL REMAIN ON THIS SHIP. I WILL DESCEND AND OBTAIN THE ARTIFACT.
THEN I WILL IDENTIFY THOSE RESPONSIBLE FOR COMPROMISING THIS OPERATION...

"...AND AFTER THEY ARE PROPERLY SHAMED, I'M GOING TO CUT THEM TO PIECES."
YOU HAVE SHOWN MOST BLESSED AIM, MY BROTHER.
AS IF THE HAND OF GOD HIMSELF GUIDED THE BOLTS' PATH...
AND NOW, IT RAINS GIFTS FROM ABOVE.
GREAT GIFTS, YOUR HOLINESS.

BEHOLD THIS BEAUTIFUL ARTIFACT...
YET MORE PROOF OF THE RIGHTEOUS-NESS OF OUR CAUSE.
JUDGMENT HAS FINALLY ARRIVED FOR THE SO-CALLED HAND OF THE DIDACT.
ONCE THE GREAT FRAUD 'MDAMA'S SINS ARE EXPOSED, HIS OWN ARMIES WILL RISE AGAINST HIM AND ALL WILL JOIN AS ONE.
THIS IS BUT THE BEGINNING, BROTHERS...
FOR I AM SALI 'NYON, THE ONE TRUE PROPHET. LET MY NAME BE SPOKEN ALL ACROSS THIS UNIVERSE.

AKTIS IV
2558-07-20 0637 SMT

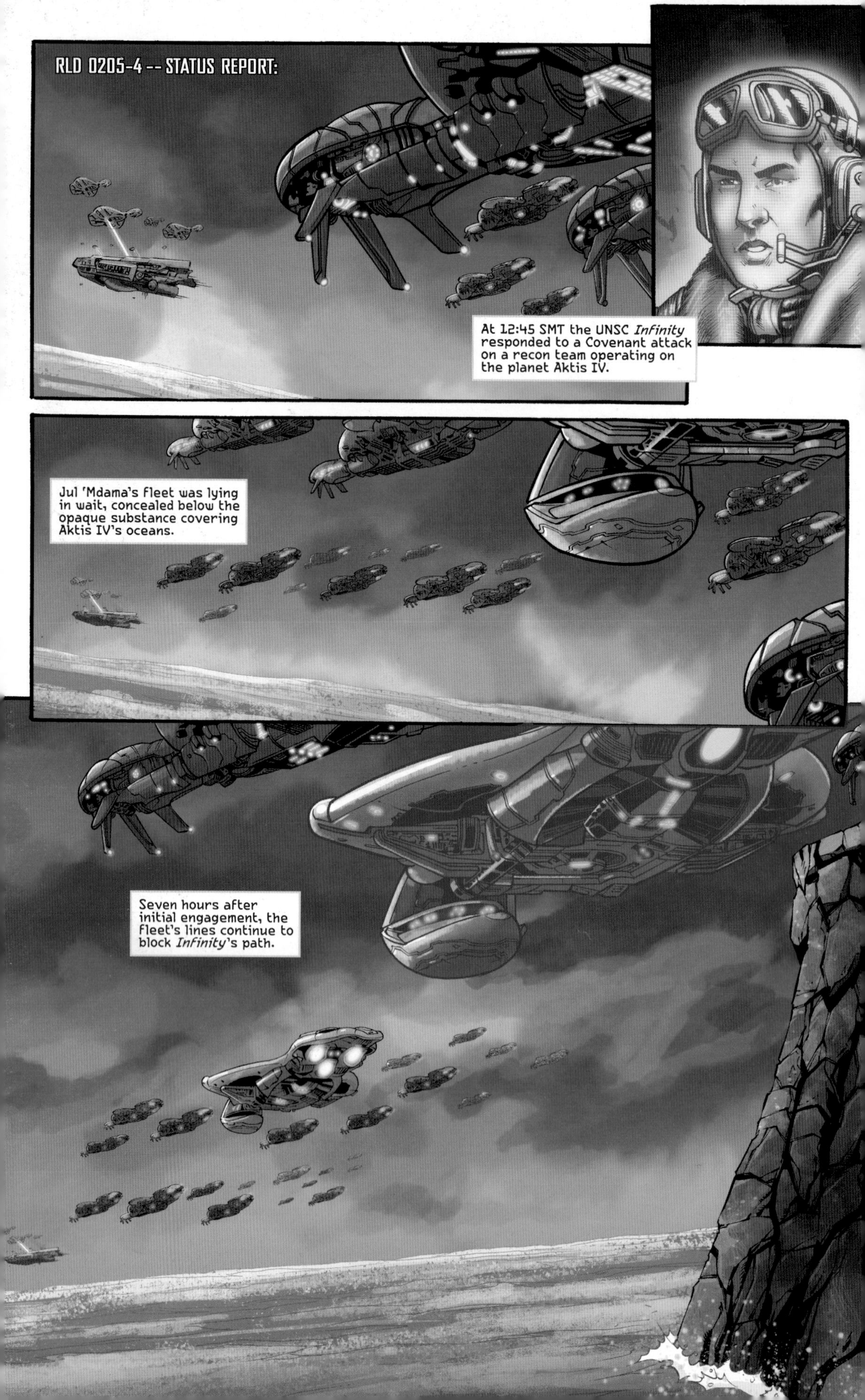

RLD 0205-4 -- STATUS REPORT:

At 12:45 SMT the UNSC *Infinity* responded to a Covenant attack on a recon team operating on the planet Aktis IV.

Jul 'Mdama's fleet was lying in wait, concealed below the opaque substance covering Aktis IV's oceans.

Seven hours after initial engagement, the fleet's lines continue to block *Infinity*'s path.

On the ground, Commander Palmer's team has established a defensive position within a recently unearthed Forerunner structure.

Shortly after *Infinity* received this message, however, all communication was lost.

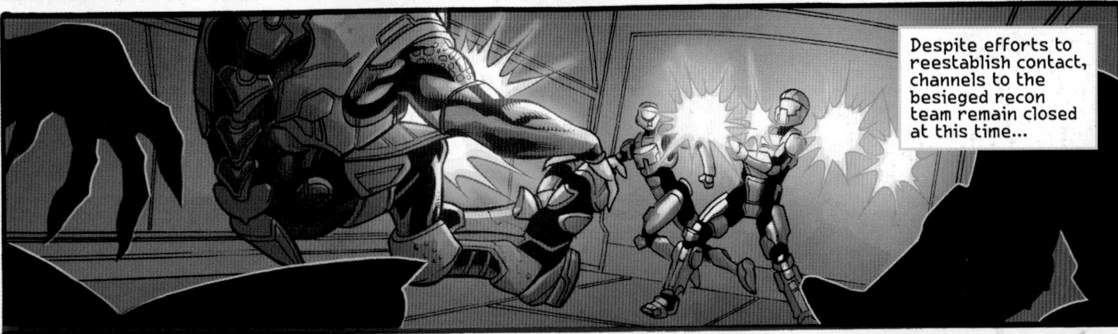

Despite efforts to reestablish contact, channels to the besieged recon team remain closed at this time...

WE GOTTA MOVE, THORNE!
WHAT'S IT LOOK LIKE I'M DOING, RAY?

NOT SURE HOW LONG THIS'LL HOLD.
I'LL WARN THE OTHERS.
COMMANDER PALMER, THIS IS THORNE...

MORE COVENANT! THEY'VE PUSHED US ALMOST ALL THE WAY BACK...
AT LEAST TELL ME YOU PICKED UP HOYA ALONG THE WAY.
AFRAID NOT.
DAMMIT.
JUST HOLD YOUR CURRENT POSITION AS LONG AS YOU CAN. I'LL CHECK IN SOON.
YOU GET THIS TRANSLOCATION GRID WORKING, I'LL TAKE BACK EVERYTHING I'VE EVER SAID ABOUT YOU, GLASSMAN.
WE MUST BE IN SERIOUS TROUBLE IF YOU'RE MAKING THAT OFFER.
THE GRID'S FULLY FUNCTIONAL, BUT BEFORE ACTIVATION, I NEED TO DECIPHER THE COORDINATES OF EXIT PORTALS.
LAST TIME, I CAME OUT THE OTHER END STARING DOWN THE BARREL OF A HUNDRED COVENANT GUNS.
THERE'S NO GUARANTEED SAFE EXIT, OF COURSE. BUT CERTAIN WAYPOINTS ARE LESS LIKELY TO BE OVERRUN BY JUL'S TROOPS THAN OTHERS.
WELL, HOW THE HELL ARE WE SUPPOSED TO FIGURE THAT OUT...

"...WHEN WE STILL DON'T HAVE ANY IDEA OF WHAT'S REALLY GOING ON UP THERE?"
ANOTHER TRAITOR?
...THEIR NUMBERS ARE GREATER THAN I'D IMAGINED.
COMMANDER 'MDAMA, I RECOMMEND YOU RETURN TO THE RETRIBUTION UNTIL WE'VE ROOTED OUT THE REST OF THEM.
NONSENSE.
BEFORE WE DETAINED THIS HERETIC, HE TRANSMITTED THIS MESSAGE ACROSS THE ENTIRE FLEET.
...FZZZZT...I AM SALI 'NYON... I SOUND THE CALL TO ALL TRUE BELIEVERS... JOIN US AS WE RISE TO DEFEAT THE IMPOSTOR 'MDAMA...FZZT...
HIS DEATH WILL MARK A NEW ERA OF GREATNESS FOR THE COVENANT, A RETURN TO OUR GLORIOUS...

SO, SALI'S FINALLY MAKING HIS MOVE...

INDEED, COMMANDER. A CAPTURED INSURGENT CONFIRMED THAT SALI IS RESPONSIBLE FOR SHOOTING DOWN THE HUMAN'S SHIP.
SALI'S TIMING WAS FORTUNATE. HIS FOLLOWERS PROBABLY SEE THAT AS SOME TYPE OF DIVINE INFLUENCE.

THE BEST WAY FOR US TO CORRECT THAT ***MISCONCEPTION*** IS TO DRAG HIS CORPSE THROUGH THE DIRT.
WHAT OF OUR PROGRESS AT THE HOLY SITE?

THE HUMANS HAVE BARRICADED THEMSELVES INSIDE, BUT WE SHOULD BE BREAKING THROUGH ANY MINUTE NOW.

WHEN YOU REACH THE INNER CHAMBER, KILL THEM ALL.
EXCEPT GLASSMAN.

I'VE GOT A SPECIAL PUNISHMENT PLANNED FOR HIM.

DOCTOR HALSEY...
I JUST HEARD THAT MANIAC'S MESSAGE.
WHO IS THIS SALI 'NYON?
AN UNEXCEPTIONAL WARRIOR AND INEPT COMMANDER.
BUT HIS DEVOTION TO THE FORERUNNERS IS TRUE, AND SOME OF OUR MORE IMPRESSIONABLE BROTHERS ARE DRAWN BY HIS FERVOR.

AS LONG AS SALI CONTINUES TO BREATHE, THE REBELLION HAS LIFE.
HE MUST BE ELIMINATED IMMEDIATELY.

JUL, NOW'S CERTAINLY *NOT* THE TIME TO BE FIGHTING A WAR ON TWO FRONTS!
INFINITY WILL EVENTUALLY BREAK YOUR LINES, AND WHEN IT *DOES* --

I AM FULLY AWARE OF THE GROWING COMPLEXITY OF THE SITUATION.

THAT IS WHY I HAVE REVISED MY DECISION TO KEEP YOU ON THE SHIP...

0815 SMT
FWOOOZ
FWOOZ
COME ON, HOYA, KEEP MOVING, MAN.
FWOOZ
KROOM KROOM
OH...

SHHTHKK
HRRRRRR...

SKREEEEEE!
ARRGHH!
HUFF
HUFF
HUFF
HUP --
SON OF A...
SSSSSSH--
KRUNCH

OKAY... OKAY...
THIS SPOT AIN'T SO BAD...
HOOOOO...
WHERE THE HELL AM I?
AND WHAT IS...
HELLOOO...

"COVIES HAVE BROKEN DOWN ANOTHER DOOR..."

HOW CLOSE ARE WE TO *EVAC?*

IF YOU'D *STOP* INTERRUPTING ME, I COULD WORK EVEN FASTER.

I JUST GOT WORD FROM *HOYA!*

HOW?

EVEN THOUGH WE CAN'T REACH *INFINITY,* COVIES LEFT A FEW CHANNELS ON THE ISLAND OPEN, PROBABLY IN THE HOPE WE'D GIVE AWAY POSITIONS.

WHAT'S HE SAY?

APPARENTLY JUL'S IN THE MIDDLE OF A *MUTINY* UP THERE. HE'S HAD TO SIC HIS KNIGHTS ON A BAND OF REBEL ELITES AND ALL HELL'S BREAKING LOOSE.

INTERESTING, SPARTAN RAY...

EVEN MORE INTERESTING, HOYA JUST SPOTTED A PHANTOM LAND IN THE MIDDLE OF THE JUNGLE...

CATHERINE HALSEY STEPPED OFF.
SHE'S UP THERE NOW, ESCORTED BY JUL'S GUARD...

STAY STRONG, BROTHER. WE'VE ARRIVED...
HHRRR... RRR...RR...
SALI 'NYON'S REBEL HIDEOUT
0831 SMT
THE GODS' JUSTICE IS INFINITE AND YOUR WISDOM GREAT, HOLY ONE...
BUT AS MORE OF OUR WOUNDED RETURN TO CAMP, I SIMPLY INQUIRE AS TO HOW WE ADDRESS THE...CURRENT CONDITION...OF THIS CAMPAIGN?
THERE IS NOTHING TO ADDRESS. THE PATH TO VICTORY IS NOT ALWAYS SO STRAIGHT.
THE FAITH OF THE TRUE BELIEVER CANNOT BE SHAKEN BY MINOR SETBACKS.
BESIDES, WHO CAN DENY OUR BLESSED FORTUNE...

WHAT MORE EVIDENCE OF THE GODS' SANCTION THAN THIS WONDROUS *GIFT?*
YET THERE IS DISTURBING EVIDENCE TO THE *CONTRARY...*
WHAT OF THE PROMETHEANS' ALLEGIANCE TO 'MDAMA?
WHY DO THE DIDACT'S WARRIORS FIGHT ON BEHALF OF THE UNHOLY? OUR BROTHERS NEED SOME KIND OF... *EXPLANATION*...FOR THE KNIGHTS' LOYALTY TO AN IMPOSTOR.
THE BEAUTY OF FAITH IS IT MAKES EXPLANATION UNNECESSARY.
ALL WILL BE REVEALED IN TIME.
NOW ALLOW ME TO ATTEND TO THOSE IN NEED OF HEALING...

HERE'S OUR SAFEST ROUTE. IT SPITS US OUT AT A SITE ON THE OTHER END OF THE ISLAND...

WHATEVER'S WAITING THERE, CAN'T IMAGINE IT'S WORSE THAN *THIS.*
SSSSZZZZZSSSSZZ
POSITIONS!
MOVE, MOVE, MOVE!

ANY OF THESE PORTALS DROP YOU INTO THE JUNGLE?
THIS ONE DOES. BUT IT'S RELATIVELY CLOSE TO OUR CURRENT LOCATION. YOU'D HAVE TO ASSUME IT'S SWARMING WITH HOSTILES.

OPEN IT.
WHAT?

DON'T WORRY, I'M NOT SENDING *YOU* THERE.
JUST OPEN ROUTES TO *BOTH* LOCATIONS! NOW!

EVAC TIME, SPARTANS!
GRAB YOUR WEAPONS AND GET YOUR ASSES UP HERE!

GRANT, YOU'RE IN CHARGE OF GLASSMAN.
WE'RE *SPLITTING* UP?
JUST FIND A SAFE AREA AND HANG ON FOR *INFINITY.*

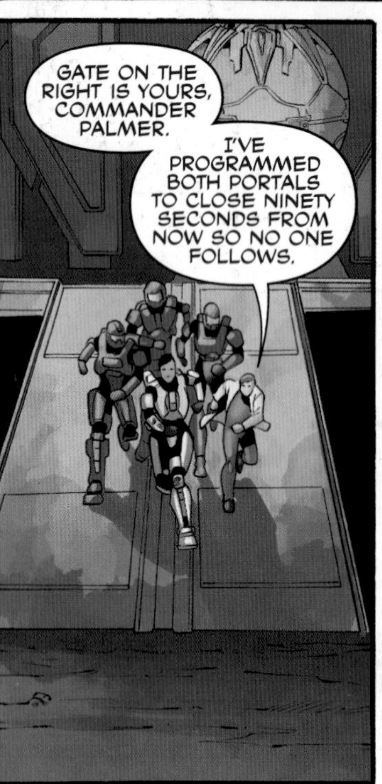

GATE ON THE RIGHT IS YOURS, COMMANDER PALMER.
I'VE PROGRAMMED BOTH PORTALS TO CLOSE NINETY SECONDS FROM NOW SO NO ONE FOLLOWS.

RAY! THORNE! HOLD UP!
YOU TWO ARE STICKING WITH ME.

THREE OF US ARE GOING ON A LITTLE *HUNT.*

FINALLY ON THE GROUND. FIRST TEAM THROUGH THE COVIE LINE.

LET'S HOPE WE'RE NOT THE LAST.

WOULDN'T CALL THIS A BEACHHEAD, BUT IT'S A START.

HEADS UP!

WE GOT A **PORTAL** OPENING AT--

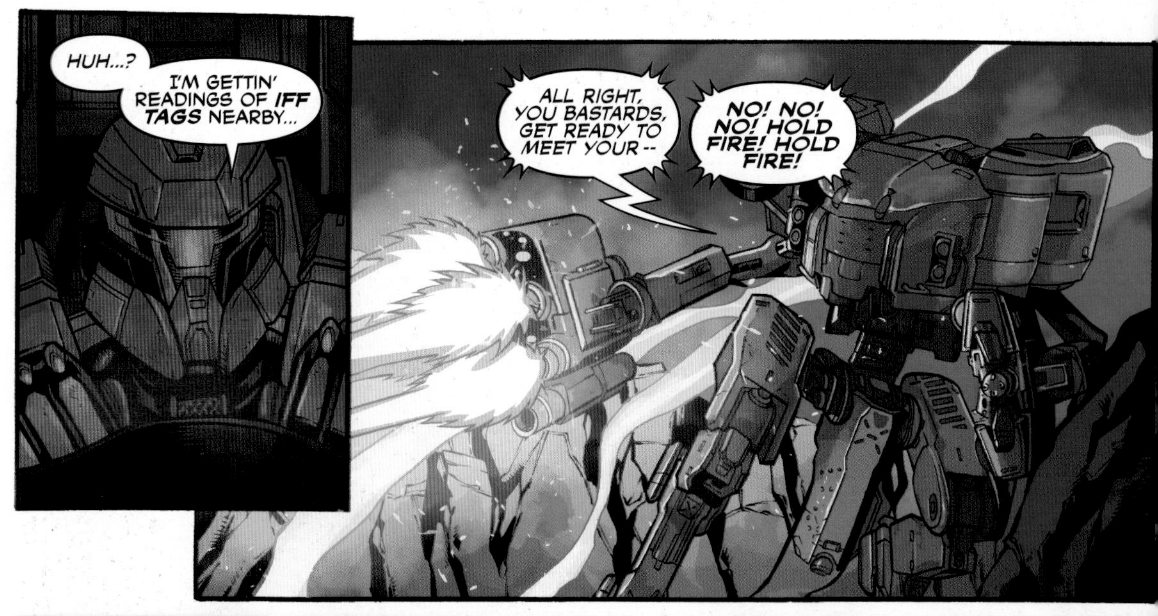
HUH...?
I'M GETTIN' READINGS OF IFF TAGS NEARBY...
ALL RIGHT, YOU BASTARDS, GET READY TO MEET YOUR --
NO! NO! NO! HOLD FIRE! HOLD FIRE!

AAHH!!

EVERYONE OKAY?

MIND TELLING US WHERE WE'RE HEADING, COMMANDER?

THE CRASH SITE. IF GLASSMAN'S MAP IS CORRECT, WE'RE ABOUT A MILE AWAY.

HOLD UP.

I HEAR SOMETHING...

THERE.

FZZZT... FZZZT...
I MUST SPEAK WITH COMMANDER 'MDAMA.
YOU WILL SPEAK WITH ME, TRAITOR...

RAY, YOU'RE MY COMMS SPECIALIST. ROUTE THE AUDIO THROUGH OUR HELMET RECORDERS.
ALREADY ON IT. I'M ACTIVATING THE TRANSLATOR...
FZZZTTT... YOU RECOGNIZE A LOST CAUSE, AND NOW YOU'D LIKE TO SWITCH SIDES...?
...RATHER CONVENIENT, IS IT NOT?
IN MY CONFUSION I ALLIED MYSELF WITH A FALSE PROPHET. BUT I NOW KNOW COMMANDER 'MDAMA IS THE ONE TRUE HAND.
FOR DIDACT'S ARMIES WOULD NEVER OBEY AN IMPOSTOR.
I ADMIT MY GUILT AND DO NOT SEEK FORGIVENESS.
BUT I WISH TO REPAIR THE DAMAGE I'VE DONE.
I WILL LEAD YOUR FORCES TO SALI 'NYON'S CAMP.
AND WHY SHOULD YOU BE TRUSTED?
BECAUSE I POSSESS AN OBJECT OF GREAT VALUE -- THE ARTIFACT SALI TOOK FROM THE WRECKAGE OF THE HUMAN'S SHIP.
I OFFER IT TO COMMANDER 'MDAMA AS A GESTURE OF MY ABSOLUTE LOYALTY.

HE'S GOT THE JANUS KEY!
SHALL I BRING IT TO YOU?

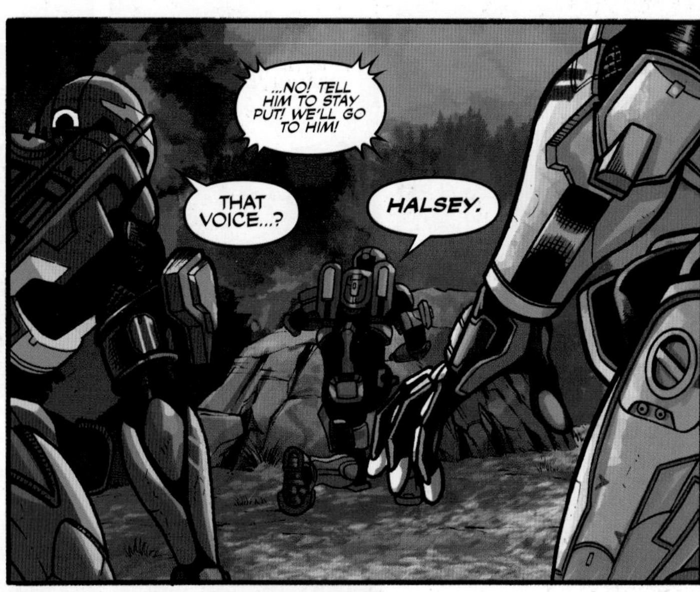

...NO! TELL HIM TO STAY PUT! WE'LL GO TO HIM!
THAT VOICE...?
HALSEY.

STAY WHERE YOU ARE. WE'VE LOCKED YOUR GENERAL COORDINATES.
CONCEAL YOURSELF AND WAIT FOR OUR NEXT CALL.
ONCE WE'VE LANDED IN THE AREA WE'LL SET A SPECIFIC RENDEZVOUS POINT.

HINGE-HEAD JUST MOVED HIS GHOST OUT OF THAT CLEARING.

HE'S HIDDEN IN THE BRUSH, BUT I STILL HAVE A GREAT SHOT.

STAND DOWN, THORNE.

ONE QUICK STRIKE AND THE KEY'S **SECURED.**
YEAH, WE'LL BE OUT OF HERE BEFORE THE COVIES HAVE ANY IDEA IT'S GONE.

YOU HEARD THAT VOICE. THE **DOCTOR'S** ON HER WAY.
AND WHEN SHE GETS HERE, WE'RE GONNA TAKE HER.

BUT THE KEY'S **RIGHT** BELOW US! WITH **ONE** COVIE GUARDING IT!
WE MOVE NOW, WE LOSE OUR CHANCE AT HALSEY.

THORNE'S **RIGHT,** COMMANDER. THREE OF US CAN EASILY TAKE THE KEY -- BUT WHO KNOWS WHAT KIND OF FORCE HALSEY'S ROLLING IN WITH?

HALSEY'S BEEN PLAYING US THIS ENTIRE TIME.

NOW SHE'S GONNA GET CAUGHT IN HER OWN DAMN TRAP.

AKTIS IV
2558-07-20 1147 SMT
ANYTHING?
NOTHING YET...

...BUT I'VE GOT A CLEAR VIEW. WE'LL HAVE A GREAT SHOT AT HALSEY WHEN SHE COMES TO COLLECT THAT KEY.
HELL OF A RISK WE'RE TAKING...
SHE'S GOT A HELL OF A LOT TO ANSWER FOR, THORNE.

JUST SAYING, THERE'S GOTTA BE SOME OTHER WAY TO --
TOO LATE TO CHANGE THE PLAN...
HOLD UP! THIS MIGHT BE IT...

YEP. SIGNAL JUST CAME IN.
HE'S ON THE MOVE.

WE'LL TAKE UP A POSITION FURTHER DOWN THE HILL BEFORE HALSEY'S PARTY ROLLS IN.

NO TIME, COMMANDER...

"THEY'RE ***HERE.***"

COMMANDER 'MDAMA, OUR CONVOY HAS MADE **CONTACT** WITH THE DEFECTOR.

JUST GET THAT ARTIFACT INTO HALSEY'S HANDS AS QUICKLY AS POSSIBLE.

ONCE SHE VERIFIES ITS AUTHENTICITY, WE'LL BE FREE TO MOVE AGAINST 'NYON WITH MORE **DECISIVE** FORCE.

THE **EXCAVATORS** ARE ALREADY IN POSITION.

GOOD. NOW **DIVERT** THOSE SUPPORT TEAMS **AWAY** FROM HALSEY.

THEY'LL BE BETTER SERVED FENDING OFF THE HUMANS' INCURSION ON THE EASTERN TIP OF THE ISLAND.

BUT IF THE SURRENDER OF THE ARTIFACT IS SOME KIND OF AMBUSH?
THE KILLING OF A HUMAN COLLABORATOR WOULD BE A GREAT MORALE BOOST FOR 'NYON'S MEN.

THERE WON'T BE ANY AMBUSH. WE'VE SLAUGHTERED NEARLY ALL OF THEM, AND THE REMAINDER HAVE TAKEN REFUGE WITH THEIR LEADER.
JUST PIVOT THOSE TEAMS TO THE MAIN FRONT. WE'RE RUNNING OUT OF TIME, BROTHER...

"Captain, Covenant ships are forming a single line..."
JUL'S MAKING HIS LAST STAND EARLIER THAN I'D EXPECTED.
WHAT'S THE LATEST ON THOSE *SURVIVORS* FROM THE RECON TEAM?
They're secured, but we can't chance an exfil until things settle down. Last I heard from Spartan Grant, she told me --
SPARTAN *GRANT?* WHERE THE HELL'S COMMANDER *PALMER?*
Apparently she ordered Glassman to translocate her to some spot near the center of the island. Took Spartans Ray and Thorne with her.
WHAT'D SHE DO *THAT* FOR?
Not sure, Captain...

"...Whatever Palmer's up to, she kept it to herself."
COMMANDER, WE'RE TOO LOW ON AMMO TO ENGAGE A FORCE THAT SIZE.
WELL, IT'S GETTING SMALLER BY THE SECOND...
"JUL MUST BE RUNNING OUT OF FIREPOWER AT THE FRONT.
"AWAY THEY GO...
"AND HERE COMES HALSEY.
"I KNEW SHE COULDN'T RESIST PUTTING HERSELF IN THE MIDDLE OF THIS."
THIS WAS LOOKING LIKE SUICIDE A COUPLE SECONDS AGO.
NOW WE MIGHT JUST PULL IT OFF.
I'M GONNA MAKE MY WAY DOWN TO THAT GHOST OUR ELITE STASHED IN THE BUSHES. KEEP AN EYE OUT AND I'LL SIGNAL WHEN I'M READY TO MOVE.
AND GATHER UP THE REST OF OUR FRAG GRENADES...

I ASSURE YOU THIS IS NO TRICK.
I COME HERE TO ATONE FOR MY SINS, NOTHING MORE.
THERE'S NO ATONING FOR WHAT YOU'VE DONE, YOU FILTHY HERETIC.

THAT'S ENOUGH.
LET HIM SHOW US WHAT HE'S GOT.

WHY IS A...HUMAN... HERE TO RECEIVE --
THESE ARE COMMANDER 'MDAMA'S ORDERS! DO AS SHE SAYS!

PERFECT.
WAIT! I --
FWOOOZ
FWOOOOZ

WHAT HAVE YOU DONE?!
WE WERE SUPPOSED TO TAKE HIM ALIVE SO HE COULD LEAD US TO HIS COMRADES!

WE DISCOVERED THEIR HIDEOUT HOURS AGO. IT'S BEING ANNIHILATED AS WE SPEAK.

WHY WASN'T I TOLD?

WHAT DOES IT MATTER? JUST FOLLOW ORDERS AND KEEP YOUR CLAWS OFF ME.
STOP IT, YOU TWO!
WE'VE GOT THE ARTIFACT, NOW LET'S GET OUT OF HERE BEFORE --

KRA-THOOM
KRA-THOOM
KRA-THOOM

WHERE ARE THEY? I DON'T SEE--
INCOMING!
HUH?

HRRRRR!

THOOM THOOM THOOM

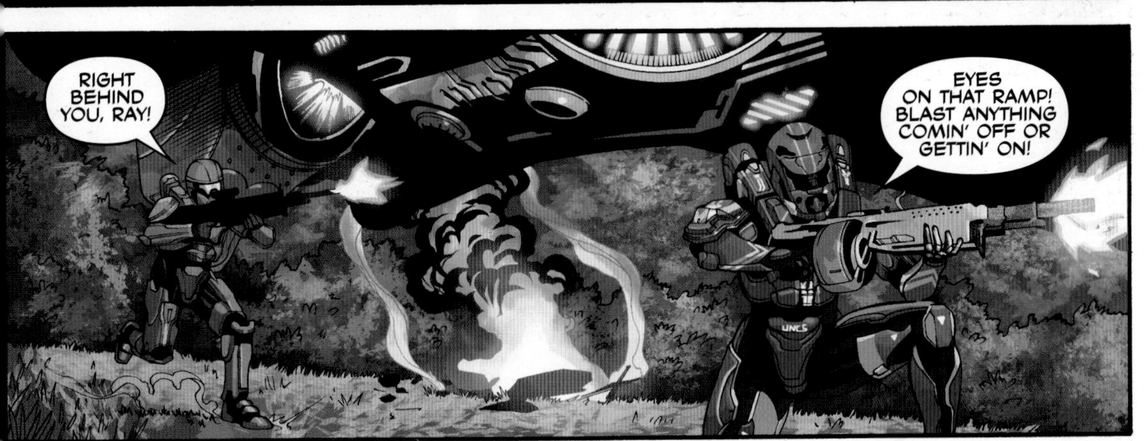

RIGHT BEHIND YOU, RAY!
EYES ON THAT RAMP! BLAST ANYTHING COMIN' OFF OR GETTIN' ON!

GET ME OUT OF HERE!
THEY'VE CUT OFF ACCESS TO THE SHIP.

TAKE HER INTO THE TREES.
I'LL CALL YOU WHEN WE'VE DEFEATED THESE THREE.

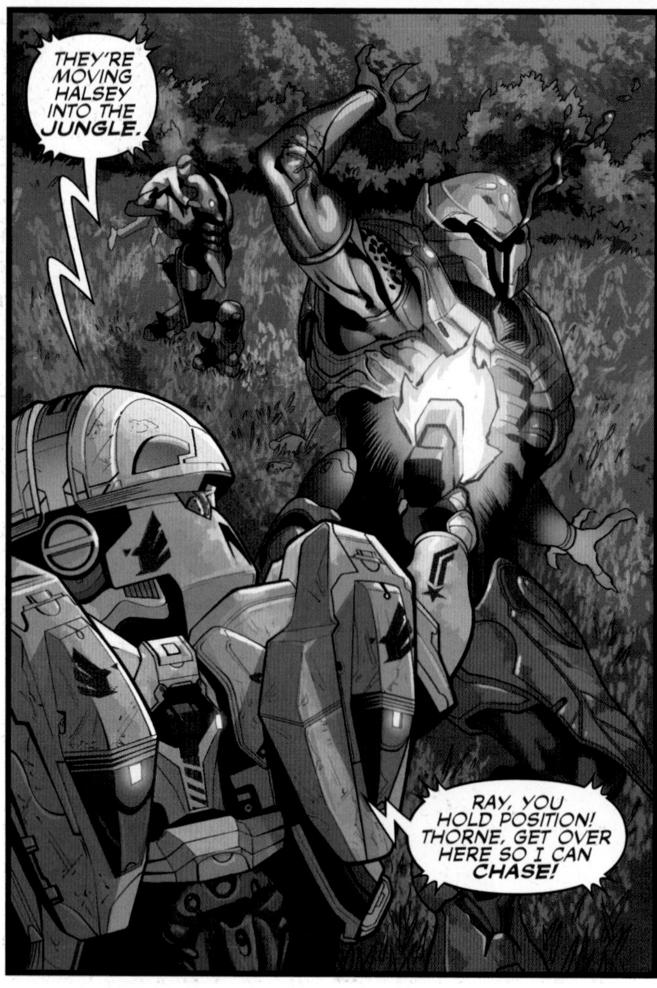
THEY'RE MOVING HALSEY INTO THE JUNGLE.
RAY, YOU HOLD POSITION! THORNE, GET OVER HERE SO I CAN CHASE!

ON MY WAY!

I'M PERFECTLY CAPABLE OF *WALKING*, YOU KNOW.
JUNGLE'S TOO THICK. I'M GOING TO HAVE TO USE MY SWORD...

I THOUGHT JUL'S FORCES STILL HAD CONTROL OF THE ISLAND. WHAT *HAPPENED* BACK THERE?
SPARTANS...

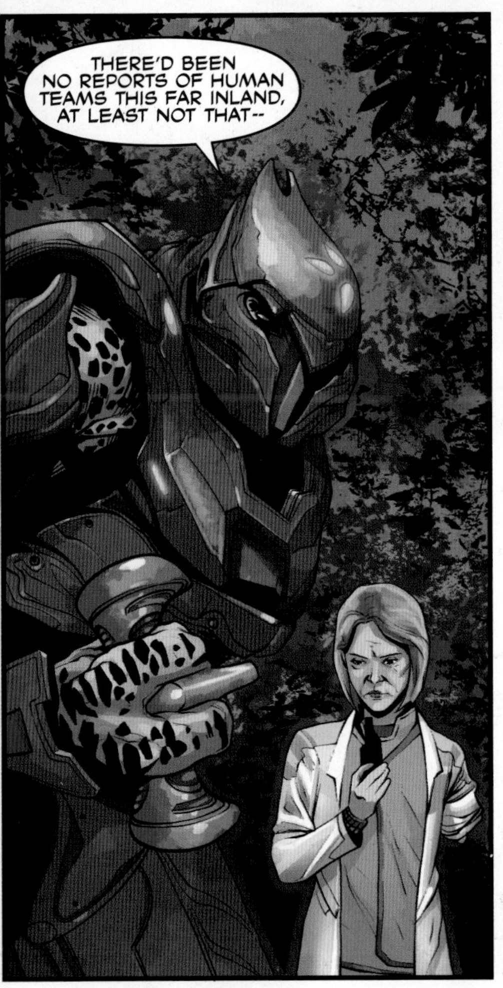
THERE'D BEEN NO REPORTS OF HUMAN TEAMS THIS FAR INLAND, AT LEAST NOT THAT--

SNAP
...

THOOM
THOOM
THOOM
THOOM

THUD

DR. HALSEY.
GREAT RUNNING INTO YOU LIKE THIS...

AKTIS IV
2558-07-20 1245 SMT
KRAAAA-
HROOOOM

THERE GOES THE LAST OF THE *HERETICS'* HIDEOUTS.
AND LOOK WHO WE CAUGHT *FLEEING* THE CAVES...

THE GREAT *TRAITOR,* SALI 'NYON.

HIS INSURRECTION COULDN'T HAVE COME AT A WORSE TIME.
HE'LL PAY DEARLY FOR THIS. KEEP HIM *ALIVE* SO I CAN--
COMMANDER 'MDAMA!

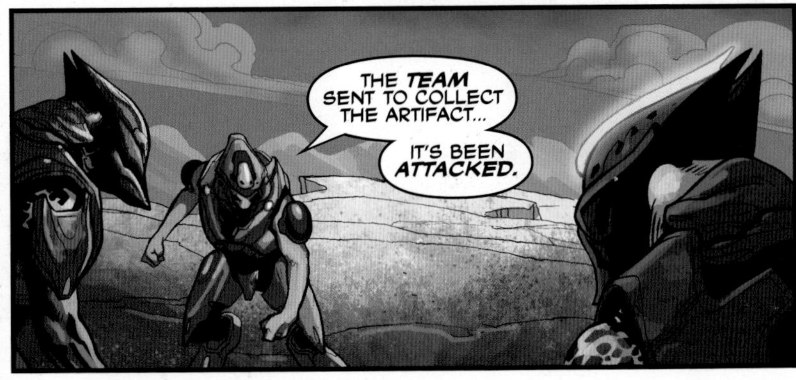
THE *TEAM* SENT TO COLLECT THE ARTIFACT...
IT'S BEEN *ATTACKED.*

1320 SMT
WHERE ARE YOU TAKING ME?
DID QUEEN OSMAN CHANGE HER MIND AGAIN, REALIZE SHE NEEDS SLAVE LABOR FOR ANOTHER PROJECT?

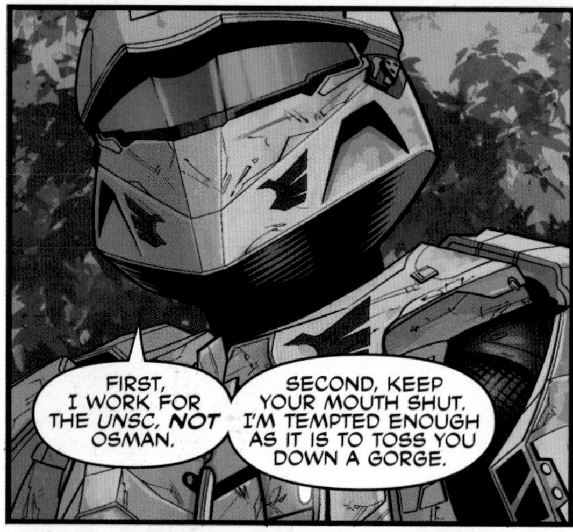
FIRST, I WORK FOR THE *UNSC*, **NOT** OSMAN.
SECOND, KEEP YOUR MOUTH SHUT. I'M TEMPTED ENOUGH AS IT IS TO TOSS YOU DOWN A GORGE.

YOU ALREADY TOOK MY **ARM.** THAT WASN'T GOOD ENOUGH FOR YOU?
AFTER YOUR **DEFECTION,** PUBLIC EXECUTION MIGHT NOT EVEN CUT IT.

IT WAS HARDLY A DEFECTION. I SIMPLY EMBRACED THE PARTY THAT WASN'T ACTIVELY TRYING TO **MURDER** ME.
UNDER THE CIRCUMSTANCES, I'D EXPECT YOU'D DO THE SAME.
IT'S ONE RATIONALIZATION AFTER ANOTHER WITH YOU.

YOU'RE A TRAITOR AND A WAR CRIMINAL. THAT'S ALL THERE IS TO IT.

IT'S AWFULLY **CONVENIENT** TO THINK OF ME THAT WAY -- ISN'T IT, PALMER?

YOU CAN'T BE THAT NAIVE.
YOU REALLY THINK I COULD HAVE PULLED OFF EVERYTHING I'VE BEEN ACCUSED OF WITHOUT THE FULL SUPPORT OF ONI? OF THE ENTIRE UNSC?

CONSIDER THE RESOURCES. THE BUDGETS. YOU THINK THOSE DECISIONS WERE MADE UNILATERALLY?
WHETHER IT WAS A SIGNED FORM OR A WINK -- THEY APPROVED IT ALL.

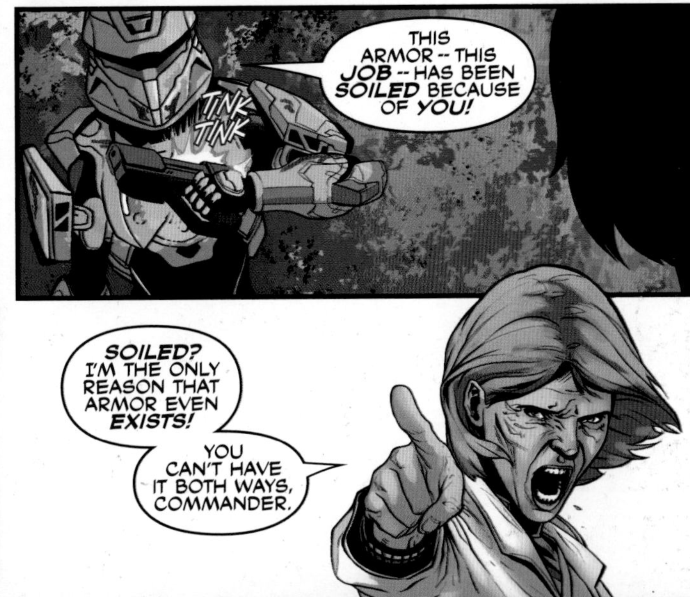
TINK TINK
THIS ARMOR -- THIS JOB -- HAS BEEN SOILED BECAUSE OF YOU!
SOILED? I'M THE ONLY REASON THAT ARMOR EVEN EXISTS!
YOU CAN'T HAVE IT BOTH WAYS, COMMANDER.

UNLESS, OF COURSE, YOU FIND THE PERFECT SCAPEGOAT.
THEN SPEND YEARS REWRITING HISTORY...

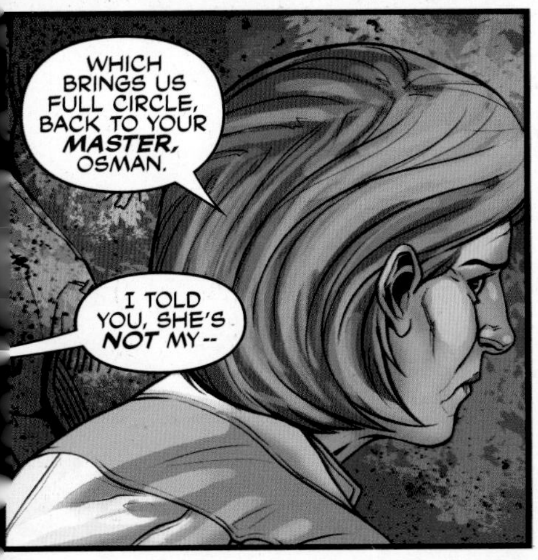
WHICH BRINGS US FULL CIRCLE, BACK TO YOUR MASTER, OSMAN.
I TOLD YOU, SHE'S NOT MY --

HEY!

OH--

HALSEY!

THOOOOOOOM

TZZSSSTTT
THUNK
SKREEEEE

HRRRRR...

beep-beep--beep
HALSEY?

GET ME DOWN FROM HERE, JUL!
THERE'S A SHIP HEADED TO RETRIEVE YOU NOW.

WE TRACKED YOU WITH THE TRANSPONDER, BUT UNTIL YOU APPEARED WE WERE UNABLE TO PINPOINT YOUR EXACT LOCATION.

WHAT OF THE SPARTAN?

DON'T WORRY ABOUT HER.
I'VE GOT WHAT WE CAME FOR.

2558-07-23 1412 SMT
(3 DAYS LATER)

UNSC INFINITY

PALMER.

CAPTAIN...?

WASN'T EXPECTING *YOU*...WHAT WITH THE *FORMALITY* OF THE SETTING.
WELL, IT'S NOT MY SHOW. WHICH IS WHY I DROPPED IN.

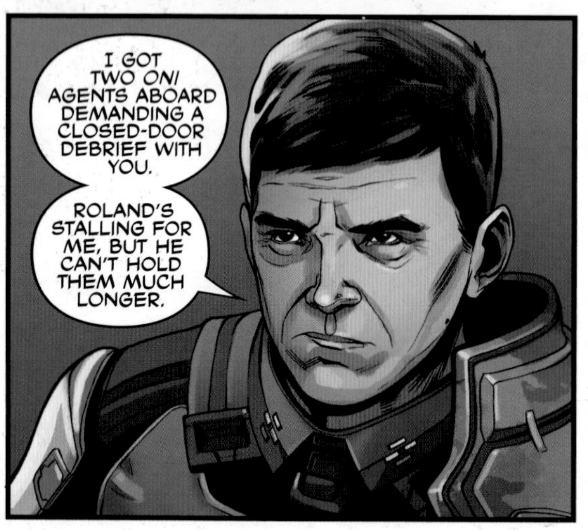

I GOT TWO *ONI* AGENTS ABOARD DEMANDING A CLOSED-DOOR DEBRIEF WITH YOU.
ROLAND'S STALLING FOR ME, BUT HE CAN'T HOLD THEM MUCH LONGER.

SO TELL ME WHAT HAPPENED.
THEN WE'LL GET YOUR STORY STRAIGHTENED OUT.

WHEN I HEARD HALSEY WAS ON THE GROUND, I HAD TO TAKE A SHOT AT HER.
IT WAS A GAMBLE. BUT I STILL BELIEVE IT WAS THE RIGHT CALL.

YOU'VE GOT A JOB AHEAD OF YOU CONVINCING YOUR SPARTANS OF THAT.
RAY AND THORNE WERE SEETHING WHEN WE FINALLY FOUND THEM.

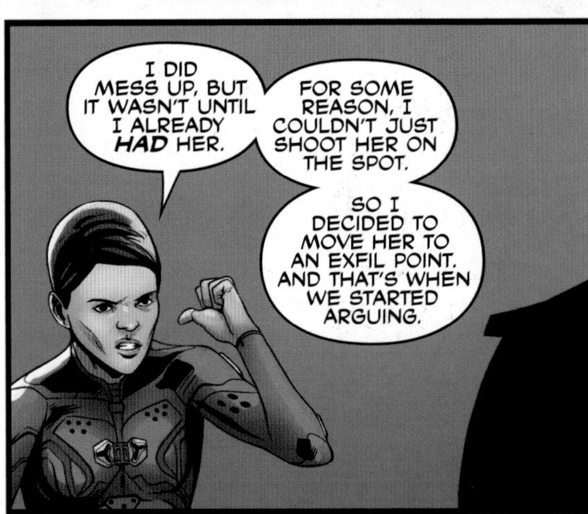
I DID MESS UP, BUT IT WASN'T UNTIL I ALREADY *HAD* HER.
FOR SOME REASON, I COULDN'T JUST SHOOT HER ON THE SPOT.
SO I DECIDED TO MOVE HER TO AN EXFIL POINT. AND THAT'S WHEN WE STARTED ARGUING.

I GOT DISTRACTED, AND SHE...

DISAPPOINTING AS IT IS, SARAH, WE CAN DEAL WITH IT.

NO, TOM...
BECAUSE I DIDN'T JUST LET HALSEY GET AWAY.
I LET HER ESCAPE *WITH* THE *ARTIFACT...*

"...WHICH MEANS SHE'S REUNITED THE TWO HALVES.
"AND IF SHE AND JUL SACRIFICED THAT MUCH TO MAKE IT HAPPEN, WE'VE GOT TO ASSUME THE WORST ABOUT WHAT THAT KEY ACTUALLY UNLOCKS..."
THERE IT IS...
OUR DESTINATION...
THE ABSOLUTE RECORD.

Illustration by Jean-Sébastien Rossbach

The year 2550: The Human-Covenant War continues to rage. Three more years of fighting remain before this brutal conflict finally winds down.

The year 2556: Though humanity survives, Earth's colonies are decimated. Small pockets of survivors struggle to rebuild their shattered worlds and defend themselves against bands of Covenant fringe groups who refuse to accept defeat.

KYNUR
CAPITAL OF THE PLANET MINAB
2550

"IT STARTS WITH FIREBALLS, A HUNDRED METERS WIDE, CRASHING DOWN FROM THE SKY.

"FOLKS AT GROUND ZERO NEVER KNOW WHAT HIT 'EM. THEY BLINK AND THEY'RE GONE.

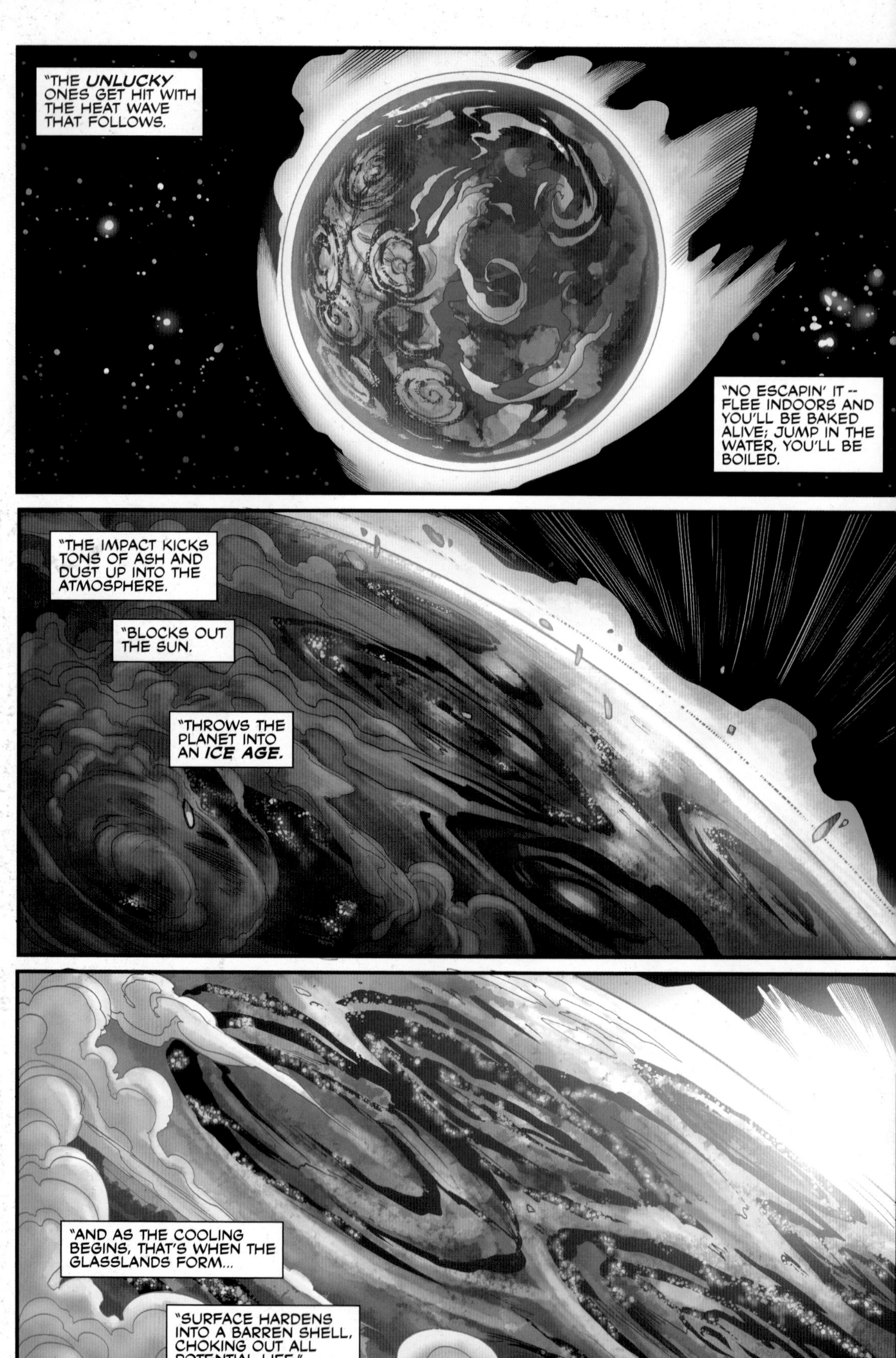
"THE UNLUCKY ONES GET HIT WITH THE HEAT WAVE THAT FOLLOWS.
"NO ESCAPIN' IT -- FLEE INDOORS AND YOU'LL BE BAKED ALIVE; JUMP IN THE WATER, YOU'LL BE BOILED.
"THE IMPACT KICKS TONS OF ASH AND DUST UP INTO THE ATMOSPHERE.
"BLOCKS OUT THE SUN.
"THROWS THE PLANET INTO AN ICE AGE.
"AND AS THE COOLING BEGINS, THAT'S WHEN THE GLASSLANDS FORM...
"SURFACE HARDENS INTO A BARREN SHELL, CHOKING OUT ALL POTENTIAL LIFE."

THE PLANET CLEYELL
2556
"THE POINT IS TO MAKE THE PLACE UNINHABITABLE.
"BUT THERE'S MORE TO IT THAN THAT.
"THEY'RE BUILDING MONUMENTS..."
UNSC CASCADIA
REMINDERS TO ALL US HERETICS OF THE PUNISHMENT THAT AWAITS US FOR THE SIN OF OUR MERE EXISTENCE.
MY GOD. I THOUGHT THESE GLASSING ATTACKS STOPPED AFTER THE WAR ENDED.
SOME COVIE FRINGE GROUPS HAVE ACTUALLY STEPPED THEM UP, TRYING TO PROVE THEY'RE STILL RELEVANT BY TERRORIZING THE OUTER COLONIES.
THIS ONE, CLEYELL, WAS RECENT. THEY HIT THE ONLY CITY LEFT ON THE PLANET.
THOSE FOLKS MADE IT ALL THE WAY THROUGH THE WAR...FOR THIS.
GENTLEMEN.
I KNOW OUR MISSION'S SUPPOSED TO BE COMPLETE, BUT WE MAY HAVE A ***SEARCH*** AND ***RESCUE*** ON OUR HANDS NOW...
THE SHIP JUST PICKED UP A DISTRESS BEACON FROM CLEYELL'S SURFACE.
ALL DUE RESPECT, SIR, WE'D BE WASTING OUR TIME.
WHEN THE GLASSING'S THAT BAD, SURVIVORS MAKE IT A ***MONTH*** AT ***MOST.***
NOT TRUE.

...HOME PLANET OF MINAB WAS GLASSED.
SURVIVORS WERE FOUND MORE THAN ***THREE YEARS*** LATER.

AND WHO THE HELL ARE YOU?

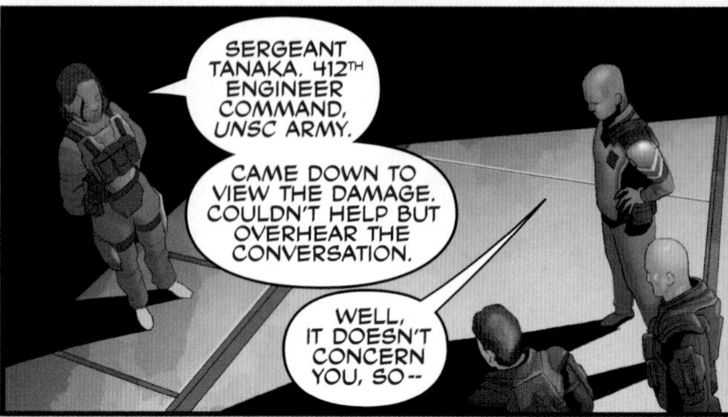

SERGEANT TANAKA. 412TH ENGINEER COMMAND, *UNSC* ARMY.
CAME DOWN TO VIEW THE DAMAGE. COULDN'T HELP BUT OVERHEAR THE CONVERSATION.
WELL, IT DOESN'T CONCERN YOU, SO--

RELAX, SOLDIER...
YOU WERE ONE OF THOSE SURVIVORS?

YES, SIR. HAPPENED TO BE WORKING ON A MINING CREW ON THE OTHER SIDE OF THE PLANET WHEN MINAB'S CAPITAL WAS HIT. ***TEN*** OF THE CREW SURVIVED THE ATTACK...
BUT WHEN SEARCH TEAMS LANDED SOME YEARS LATER, THAT NUMBER WAS DOWN TO ***THREE.***

CONDITIONS MUST HAVE BEEN ABSOLUTE ***HELL*** TO KILL THAT MANY OF THE SURVIVING PARTY.

WASN'T THE CONDITIONS DID THE KILLING...

MINAB 2551

"...IT WAS SOMETHIN' MUCH *WORSE.*"

HOLLY, YOUR FATHER'S BEEN LOOKIN' FOR YOU.
YOU TELL HIM I WAS OUT GETTIN' HIS DAMN DINNER?

HAD ME WORRIED THERE, HOLLY...

WENT TO CLEAN THE TRAPS, DAD...

GOTTA GET OUT ONCE IN A WHILE, RIGHT?
NOT LIKE WE'RE ON A TIGHT SCHEDULE ANYMORE.

STILL, I'D LIKE TO PULL APART ANOTHER ONE OF THE RIGS AS SOON AS WE CAN.
YOU'VE BECOME MY BEST ENGINEER, HOLLY, AND I NEED YOU TO HELP ME COBBLE TOGETHER A BACKUP FUSION REACTOR...

BOSS, YOU GOTTA GET DOWN HERE...
NOW.

THIS AGAIN...

WE'VE NO RIGHT TO TREAT HIM LIKE SOME RABID ANIMAL!
LIKE?! THAT'S WHAT HE IS!
WE WAIT TILL HE HAS ANOTHER LITTLE EPISODE, SOMEONE'S GONNA END UP DEAD!

HE'S SICK!
YEAH, THAT'S WHAT YOU DON'T SEEM TO UNDERSTAND.
WHAT'S THE PROBLEM?

SEE FOR YOURSELF...
HRRRRMM! HRRRRR! HRRRRM!

SO, IT'S COME TO THIS...
IT'S ONLY TEMPORARY. WE'VE ALREADY SETTLED ON THE PERMANENT SOLUTION.

RESTRAIN HIM, FINE! BUT YOU CANNOT EXECUTE THIS MAN! HE DOESN'T DESERVE--
YOU JUST DON'T GIVE A DAMN BECAUSE IT'S NOT YOU WHO LOST AN EYE!

SHAME HE DIDN'T TAKE THAT TORCH TO YOUR TONGUE INSTEAD...

WHAT'D YOU JUST SAY?!
THAT IS NOT HELPING!
PLEASE! EVERYONE, PLEASE CALM DOWN...

"LET'S TAKE THE NIGHT TO COOL OFF. TALK ABOUT IT AGAIN IN THE MORNING."
HRRRR... HRRR... HRRR...
STILL AGAINST THE IDEA OF THE DISTRESS BEACON?
COULDN'T KNOW WHAT WE'D ATTRACT.
WE'RE SAFE ENOUGH UP HERE, BUT I'D BET JACKAL SCAVENGER GANGS ARE ALREADY AT WORK, TEARING UP WHAT'S LEFT OF THE CITIES.

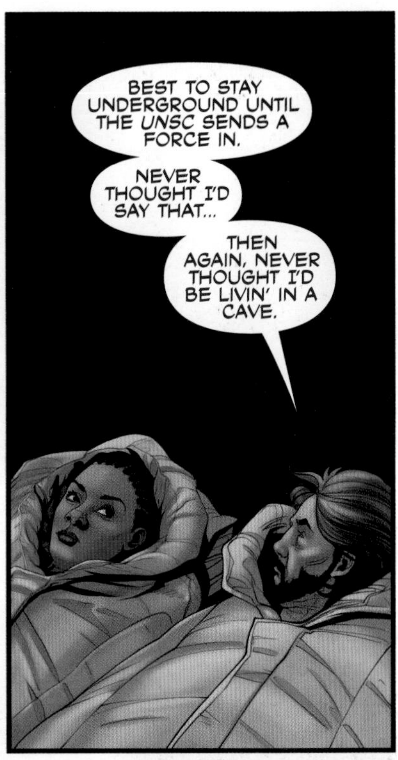
BEST TO STAY UNDERGROUND UNTIL THE UNSC SENDS A FORCE IN.
NEVER THOUGHT I'D SAY THAT...
THEN AGAIN, NEVER THOUGHT I'D BE LIVIN' IN A CAVE.

I FEEL LUCKY.
FEELS WRONG TO ADMIT IT...
Y'KNOW... WITH MOM AND THE BOYS GONE.

HOLLY, DON'T THINK ABOUT THAT STUFF.
JUST FOCUS ON THAT REACTOR YOU'RE GONNA BUILD FOR ME.

SURE, DAD.
BETTER YET, SEE IF YOU CAN'T GIVE THAT BRAIN A REST.
I NEED YOU SHARP...

"...I GOT A FEELIN' TOMORROW'S GONNA BE A ROUGH ONE."
WHO DID THIS?!
WHO CUT HIM LOOSE?!

I TOLD YOU I'D RESPECT THE AGREEMENT AS LONG AS YOU DIDN'T KILL HIM.

HEY! HEY!
WHAT?

WAS IT YOU? WAS IT?
YOU GOT NO RIGHT TO QUESTION ME.
NOW BEAT IT UNLESS YOU WANT ME TO FINISH WHAT HE STARTED...

LITTLE SHERIFF'S POSSE PLAYIN' WITH GUNS, HUH?
WHA --

NOT SO FUN NOW.
KA-THOOM

THAT'S ENOUGH.
GIVE BACK HER RIFLE.

CHECK THIS OUT.
BOSS-MAN'S LITTLE ENFORCER.

Y'ALL NEED TO TAKE A BREATH, THEN GET BACK TO WORK.
WITH THAT MANIAC ON THE LOOSE?!

WE'VE GOT TO FIND HIM!
WE'LL SPLIT UP INTO--

I'LL SWEEP THE COMPOUND ***MYSELF.***
I DON'T FIND HIM, CONSIDER THE MATTER ***CLOSED...***

"...'CAUSE IF HE'S RUNNIN' AROUND OUT THERE, THE MAN'S ALREADY DEAD."

HHHHRRRR... HHHRRR... HRRR...

HOURS LATER
DAD...
WHAT DO YOU KNOW ABOUT THESE TWO?

"THEY VALUE THEIR PRIVACY.
"NOT ALL THAT STRANGE IN THIS LINE OF WORK..."

ALL MY YEARS, I MET VERY FEW OF US TUNNEL RATS THAT YOU'D CALL THE SOCIAL TYPE.
BUT THOSE BOYS DO HAVE A PARTICULAR EDGE TO 'EM.

HERE. FIX THIS...
THEY'RE OUTER OUTER COLONY. CAN TELL FROM THE ATTITUDE.
HARDCORE MILITIA TYPES?

ROUGH TIMES CREATE ROUGH MEN, HOLLY.
BUT DO YOU THINK THEY LET THAT MAN FREE?
I MEAN, WHY WOULD THEY?

HOLLY, I --
BOSS! BOSS!

NO... NO...NO...
"I DON'T UNDERSTAND -- WHAT ARE YOU TRYING TO TELL ME?"
"LOCKDOWN! LOCKDOWN!
"LOCK IT ALL DOWN! NOW!"

GO! GO! GO!
WEEOOO WEEOOO
WEEOOO

MOVE THAT RIG! BLOCK THE GATE!
RRRRRRM
RRRMMM
RRRRMMM

THOOOOOM

FWOOOZ
FWOOOZ
FWOOOZ

DAD! WHAT ARE YOU DOING!
GO BACK, HOLLY! I'LL MEET YOU AT THE SOUTH TUNNEL!

HHSSSTTT!

KA-THOOM
SKREEEE!

FWOOZ
FWOOZ

HRRRR... HRRRR...

KLANG

WHIRRRRRRRRRRRR

HRRR!

DAD...

DAD'S GONE, LITTLE ONE.

MMMM...
MMMM...

UNSC CASCADIA
ALL DUE RESPECT, COMMANDER... RIGHT THING TO DO IS ANSWER THAT CALL.
MAY NOT MEAN MUCH TO THE *UNSC* TO HEAD OUT ON A MISSION LIKE THIS.
BUT IF ***SOMEONE'S*** ALIVE DOWN THERE, IT'LL MEAN ***EVERYTHING*** TO ***THEM.***

THAT'S SAD AND ALL, BUT IT DOESN'T CHANGE--
SHUT YOUR MOUTH, SON.

ALL RIGHT, TANAKA, YOU'VE CONVINCED ME.
WE'LL ***GO.***

AND SINCE YOU'RE THE ***EXPERT*** HERE-- ***YOU'RE*** COMING ***TOO.***

2556
UNSC CASCADIA,
STATUS REPORT

4:05 SMT: Dropship deployed to investigate distress signal on the glassed planet of Cleyell. Search team informed of potential presence of Kig-Yar scavengers.

COORDINATES LOCKED ON **BEACON.**
INITIATING FINAL APPROACH.
ANOTHER SOFT INSERTION.
MIGHT AS WELL HAVE DAMN WATERFALL NOISES PLAYIN' OVER THE RADIO.

THIS AIN'T NO LIFE FOR A HELLJUMPER.
NOT EVERYTHING STARTS QUIET STAYS THAT WAY. COULD BE A LOAD OF TROUBLE'S WAITING DOWN THERE.
LET'S HOPE.

AND LET'S HOPE THE ***SERGEANT*** HERE KNOWS WHAT SHE'S GOT HERSELF INTO.
NOT SURE HOW MUCH COMBAT SHE'S SEEN IN THE ENGINEER CORPS...

WHADDYA SAY, ***TANAKA...***
WHEN IT KICKS OFF DOWN THERE, YOU GONNA KNOW WHAT TO DO WITH THAT ***RIFLE?***

THE PLANET MINAB
SOMEWHERE IN THE HIGHLANDS
2551
TANAKA! HEY!
I'M TALKIN' TO YOU!

THREE DAYS. HASN'T UTTERED A SINGLE WORD IN THREE DAYS...

JUST GO AHEAD AND GET IT OVER WITH.

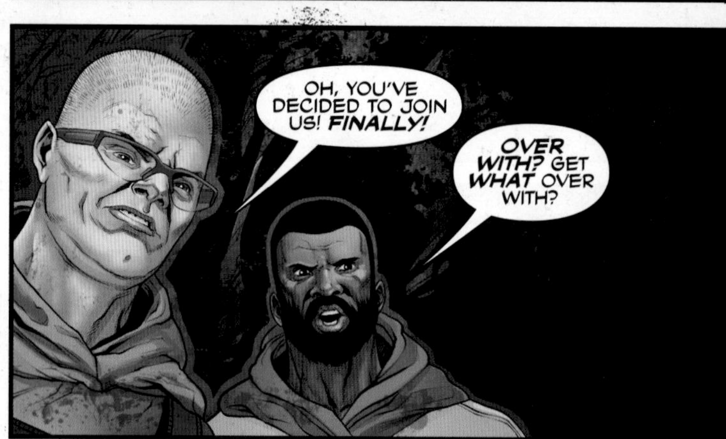
OH, YOU'VE DECIDED TO JOIN US! FINALLY!
OVER WITH? GET WHAT OVER WITH?

YOU KNOW... WHATEVER IT IS YOU'RE GONNA...

I RESENT THE IMPLICATION, SWEETHEART.
YOU MUST NOT REMEMBER CORRECTLY, BUT WE'RE THE ONLY REASON YOU'RE STILL ALIVE.

YOU'RE THE REASON EVERYONE'S *DEAD!*
IF *YOU* HADN'T FREED THAT *MANIAC,* HE WOULDA NEVER RUN AWAY, LED THOSE JACKALS TO OUR HIDEOUT!

HATE TO BREAK THE NEWS, BUT YOUR *FATHER* FREED THAT MAN.
THAT'S... THAT'S A *LIE!*

YOU BUNKED UP IN THE CAB WITH HIM...YOU MUST HAVE HEARD HIM GET UP, HEAD DOWN TO THE MAIN FLOOR THAT NIGHT?
DIDN'T SEEM STRANGE TO YOU?

MY FATHER WOULD *NEVER* -- IT MAKES *NO* SENSE!

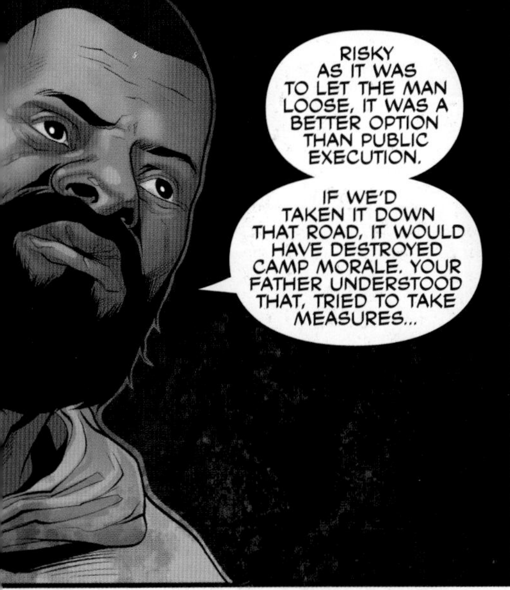
RISKY AS IT WAS TO LET THE MAN LOOSE, IT WAS A BETTER OPTION THAN PUBLIC EXECUTION.
IF WE'D TAKEN IT DOWN THAT ROAD, IT WOULD HAVE DESTROYED CAMP MORALE. YOUR FATHER UNDERSTOOD THAT, TRIED TO TAKE MEASURES...

THINGS JUST BACKFIRED ON HIM.
WASN'T HIS FAULT. WASN'T ANYONE'S FAULT.

GLAD WE CLEARED *THAT* UP, 'CAUSE WE GOT A MORE PRESSING *TOPIC* TO DISCUSS.

WE'RE NOT GONNA SURVIVE MUCH LONGER WITHOUT PROPER ***GEAR.***

"LAST YEAR WE STORED AN ***EMERGENCY CACHE*** BY AN OUTCROPPING NEAR THE CAVE. INSURANCE POLICY IN CASE THINGS GOT NASTY.

"TIME'S COME TO PICK IT UP."

"WHAT ABOUT THOSE JACKALS?"
"EVEN MORE OF 'EM NOW. AND THEY'VE SET UP CAMP RIGHT ON THE COMPOUND'S DOORSTEP."
"THEN THERE'S NO WAY WE'LL BE ABLE TO --"

TANAKA, YOU EVER HEAR STORIES ABOUT THOSE DAMNED COLONIAL INSURGENTS?
YOU KNOW, THOSE MEN AND WOMEN FIGHTIN' IN SHADOWS AND MAKIN' THE UNSC'S LIFE HELL?

WELL, YOU'RE LOOKING AT TWO OF THE BEST.
TIME FOR YOUR CRASH COURSE IN ASYMMETRIC WARFARE.

CLEYELL
2556
GETTING A STRONG SIGNAL.
THAT *TRANSMITTER* MUST BE CLOSE.

MAYBE ALL THIS ASH IS MESSING WITH THE RECEIVER, 'CAUSE I'M NOT SEEING ANYTHING AROUND HERE.

FOUND IT.
WAS WEDGED DOWN IN THIS CRACK.

WHY STASH THE TRANSMITTER *THERE?* IT DOESN'T MAKE SENSE.
DOES IF A PERSON HAS NOWHERE TO HIDE IT ON THE BODY...

HEY. TAKE A LOOK...

FRESH CORPSE... PLASMA BURNS...
TANAKA MIGHT BE ONTO SOMETHING.

MINAB 2551
"WE GOT A WAY TO COVER SCENT, TOO.
"YOU FOLLOW MY MAN'S LEAD, YOU'LL BE INVISIBLE.

"SURE, THESE JACKALS ARE STRONG AND QUICK.
"BUT WHEN IT COMES TO DRAWIN' 'EM IN, THEY'RE NO DIFFERENT THAN HUMANS.

"THEY MAKE THE SAME *MISTAKES.*
"OVERPLAY THEIR ADVANTAGES...

"GET SO FILLED WITH BLOOD LUST THEY LOSE TRACK OF THEIR SURROUNDINGS..."

KA-THOOM

"FORGET THAT THOSE WEAPONS THEY JUST PLUCKED OFF SOME POOR BASTARD'S CORPSE...

"...ARE JUST WAITING THERE TO BE TAKEN FROM THEIR OWN.

"AND WHILE ANY *ONE* OF THESE MISTAKES CAN BE ***DISASTROUS...***

"...THE COMBINATION OF ALL THREE IS INEVITABLY **FATAL.**"
EEEEEEKROOOOM
AK!

"SO THAT'S THE **STRATEGY.**

"DO IT **RIGHT** BY GIVING THE ENEMY THE OPPORTUNITY TO GET IT **WRONG.**"

THIS IS EVERYTHING.
COMPASS, PURIFICATION PUMP, AMMO, ANTIBIOTICS...

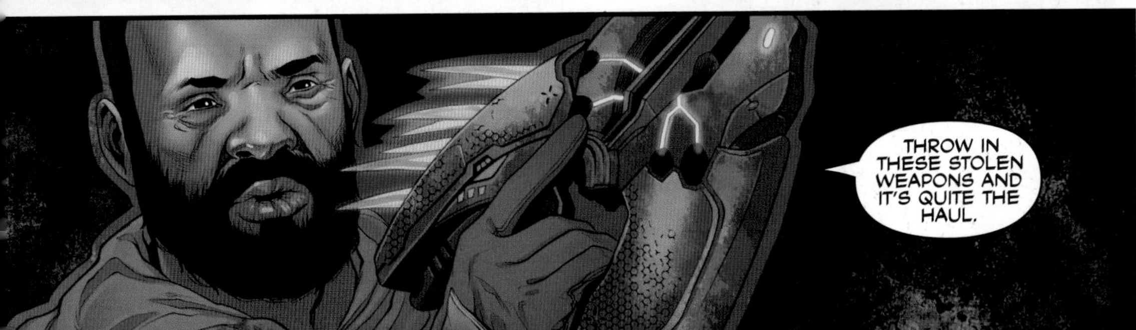
THROW IN THESE STOLEN WEAPONS AND IT'S QUITE THE HAUL.

HOW LONG TILL WE GO BACK?

NEVER.
THING LIKE THAT, YOU ONLY DO *ONCE.*

BUT WE CAN SURELY FIND A WAY INSIDE THE COMPOUND!
WE HAVE TO KNOW IF ANYONE'S STILL *ALIVE,* AND IF THEY ARE --

THERE AREN'T ANY SURVIVORS.
EVEN IF THERE WERE, JOB LIKE THAT IS NEAR IMPOSSIBLE. EVERYTHING WENT OUR WAY TONIGHT. CAN'T COUNT ON GETTIN' THAT LUCKY AGAIN.

I'LL GO BACK BY MYSELF, THEN!
WHOA THERE...
AND I'M ENTITLED TO SOME OF THAT GEAR! IT'S ONLY FAIR!

DOESN'T WORK LIKE THAT.
LISTEN, I GOT AN IDEA. JUST HEAR ME --

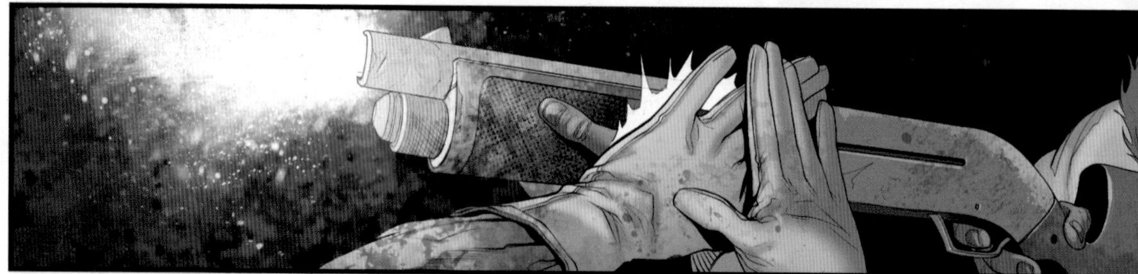

STUPID. STUPID. STUPID.
YOU BETTER HOPE THE WEATHER'S REAL NOISY TONIGHT. OTHERWISE YOU JUST LED THOSE JACKALS RIGHT TO US.

...WHAT DOES IT MATTER...JUST GIVIN' UP ANYWAY...

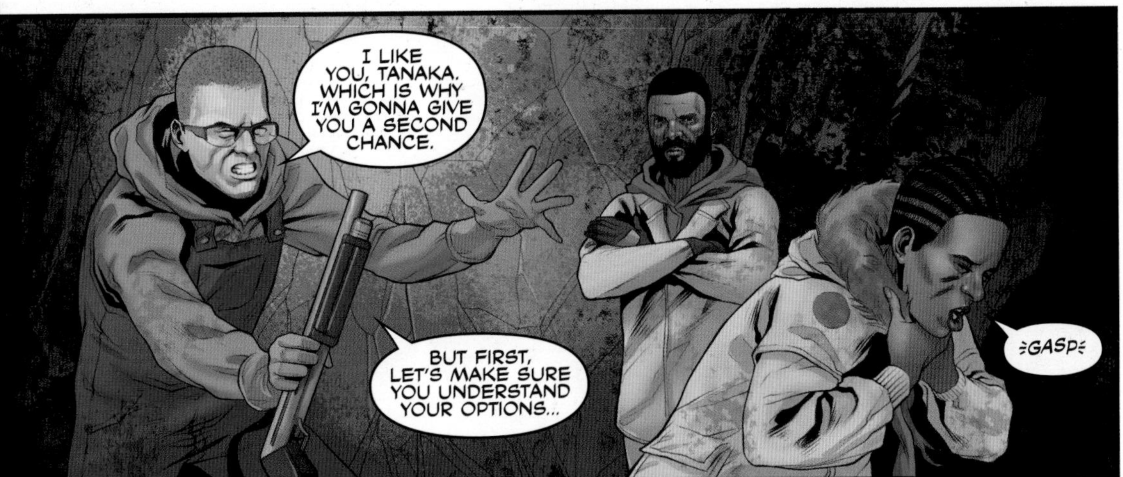
I LIKE YOU, TANAKA. WHICH IS WHY I'M GONNA GIVE YOU A SECOND CHANCE.
BUT FIRST, LET'S MAKE SURE YOU UNDERSTAND YOUR OPTIONS...
GASP

YOU EITHER JOIN US ON OUR TRIP DOWN SOUTH...
OR IT ALL ENDS FOR YOU, RIGHT HERE.

BECAUSE YOU WILL ***NOT*** BE PUTTING ***US*** IN JEOPARDY BY RUNNING OFF AND CHASING GHOSTS.

NOW GET IT TOGETHER, 'CAUSE WE GOT ***WALKIN'*** AHEAD.
MUST BE SOME OTHER SURVIVOR CAMPS OUT THERE...

FOUR MONTHS LATER...
"...WE JUST GOTTA GO *FIND* 'EM."
IF I'VE BEEN STEERIN' US RIGHT, WE'LL BE PASSIN' OUT OF THE HIGHLANDS SOON.
CREST UP AHEAD SHOULD GIVE US OUR FIRST LOOK AT THE CENTRAL PLAINS.

MY *GOD*...

ALL THAT FARMLAND, GONE.

IT'S JUST LIKE EVERYTHING FROZE. NOT IN ICE, BUT...

"...GLASS."
CLEYELL
2556
"NICE TO FINALLY GET A VIEW OF THE LAND NOW THE STORM'S CLEARED.
"WHAT ARE WE LOOKING AT HERE?"
"AGRICULTURAL STATION.
"RARE FOR A STRUCTURE TO SURVIVE THIS INTACT, BUT IT HAPPENS..."
02

...COMBINATION OF LOW-ORBIT BOMBARDMENT AND A LOCATION JUST THE RIGHT DISTANCE FROM THE BLAST ZONE.
SO *THAT'S* WHERE OUR JACKALS ARE HIDING...

CERTAINLY HAVE A FEW SHOOTERS POSITIONED ON IT.
LANDMARK LIKE THIS IS GOOD FOR LURIN' WANDERERS, BUT TOO EASY A TARGET IF ANYTHING HEAVY ROLLS IN.

THE NEST ITSELF IS SOMEWHERE *BELOW.*
THAT MAN WHO SENT THE SIGNAL...HE WOULDA NEVER ESCAPED ACROSS THAT WIDE-OPEN PLAIN. HAD TO COME FROM *BENEATH.*
CAVES.
SAW A WAY IN, ABOUT HALF A KLICK BACK.

AND THEN WHAT? *YOU* GONNA GUIDE US THROUGH?
SHOULDN'T BE A PROBLEM...

"...LIVE DOWN THERE LONG ENOUGH, THEY'RE NOT SO HARD TO NAVIGATE."
WE SHOULD BE RUNNING INTO THE SUNKEN PART OF THE STATION SOON.
SENSORS ARE LIGHTING UP LIKE CRAZY...
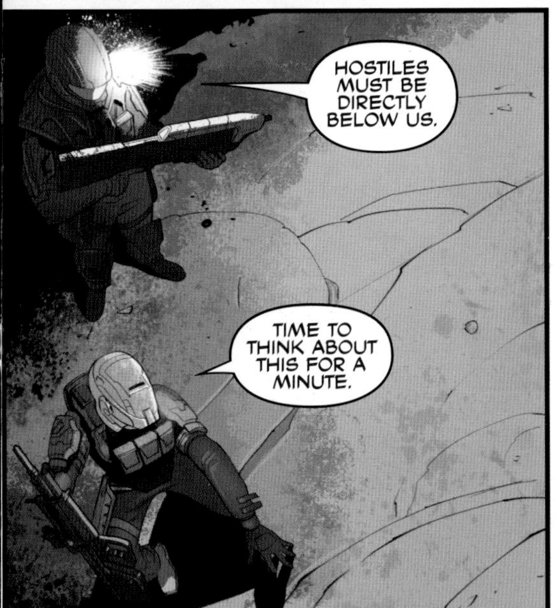
HOSTILES MUST BE DIRECTLY BELOW US.
TIME TO THINK ABOUT THIS FOR A MINUTE.

MOST IMPORTANT THING IS TO GO IN QUIET.
JACKALS SEE ANYONE COMIN', THEY'LL EXECUTE THOSE PRISONERS BEFORE THEY CAN BE FREED.
O+

BETCHA THERE'S AN ACCESS TUNNEL SOMEWHERE ALONG THAT FAR WALL...

WATCH IT! THAT GROUND'S TOO BRITTLE TO--

KRAAAAKKKK

DON'T FALL--
YOW!
FWOOZ
FWOOZ
FWOOZ

FWOOZ
FWOOZ

THUNK
--UUF!
HOLD ON!

BRAKKA
BRAKKA
BRAKKA
--AK!

FWOOZ

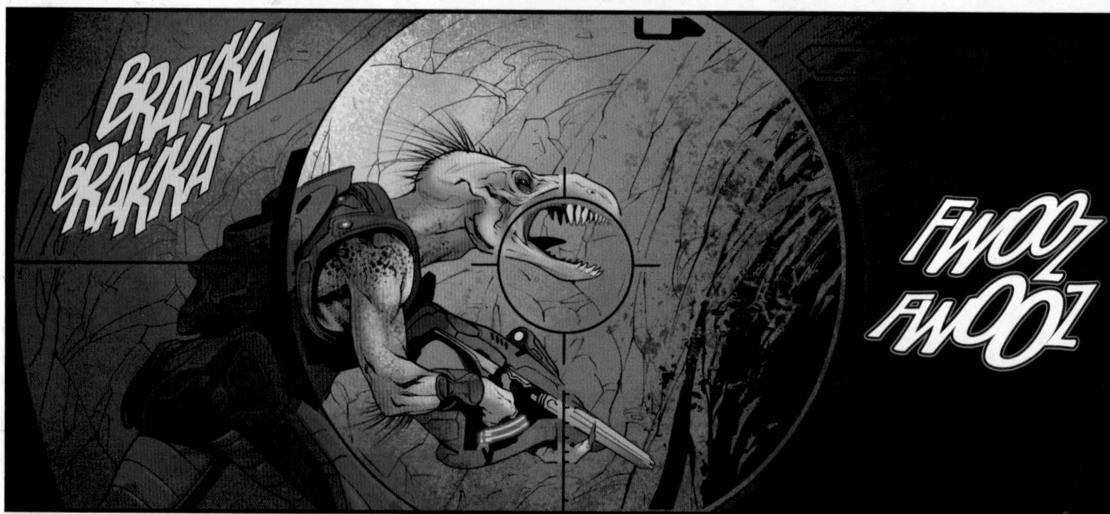
BRAKKA
BRAKKA
FWOOZ
FWOOZ

FWOOZ
FWOOZ
THOOM

HEH...

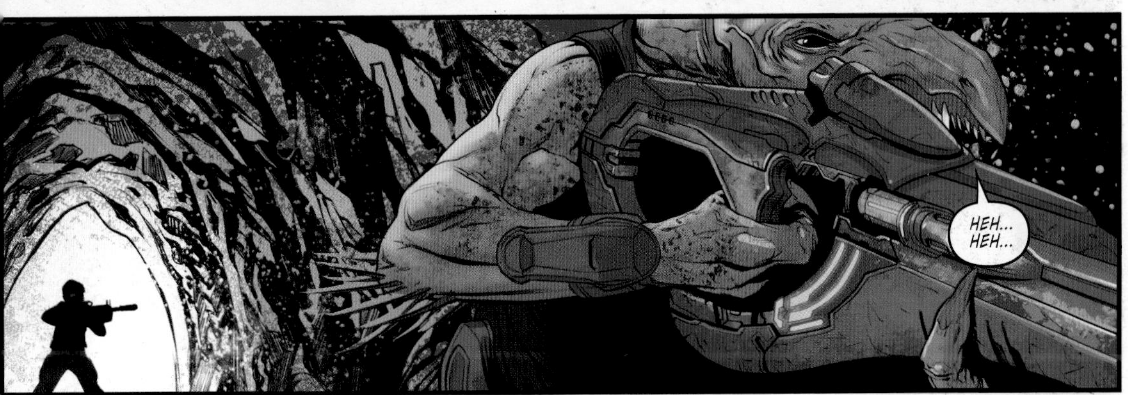
HEH...
HEH...

THOOM
UNSC

HANG ON.
BE OUT OF THERE IN NO TIME AT ALL...

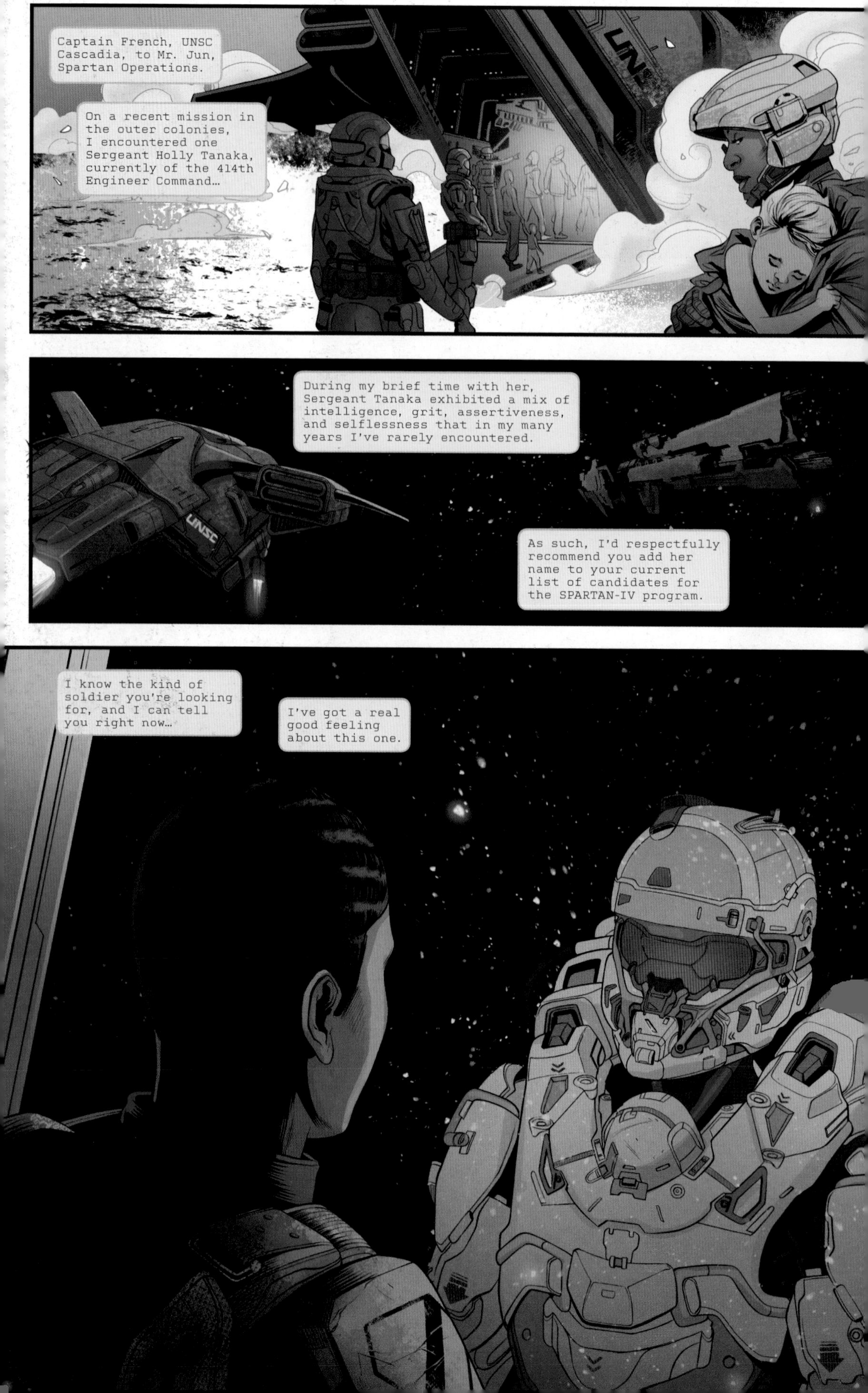

Captain French, UNSC Cascadia, to Mr. Jun, Spartan Operations.

On a recent mission in the outer colonies, I encountered one Sergeant Holly Tanaka, currently of the 414th Engineer Command…

During my brief time with her, Sergeant Tanaka exhibited a mix of intelligence, grit, assertiveness, and selflessness that in my many years I've rarely encountered.

As such, I'd respectfully recommend you add her name to your current list of candidates for the SPARTAN-IV program.

I know the kind of soldier you're looking for, and I can tell you right now…

I've got a real good feeling about this one.

Illustration by Sparth

Illustration by Jean-Sébastien Rossbach